Predictive Innovation®
Core Skills

By Mark Proffitt

ISBN: 978-0-578-11728-7

First Published in United States of America 2012 by

Mark Proffitt

Jackson, MI 49203

www.MarkProffitt.com

Table of Contents

1. Acknowledgments

My unending gratitude goes to Len Kaplan for wisdom, hard work, and dedication in developing Predictive Innovation. It is the result of his life-long work, which he has not received the credit nor reward he greatly deserves.

Thanks to my Grandmother Martha who, when I was 5 and begged to learn how to read, taught me the system of sounding out the letters. That insight started me on seeking the system behind everything.

Also gratitude to my parents for allowing me the freedom to pursue a real education without school. Without that freedom I would never have gained the knowledge or retained the sanity needed to produce anything of value.

Predictive Innovation incorporates discoveries from very many people who refused to conform and looked for the elegant system responsible for the amazing complexity of the universe. I encourage you to explore their works to help you expand your abilities with Predictive Innovation.

W. Edwards Deming, Statistical Process Control; Genrich Altshuller, TRIZ; Fritz Zwicky, Morphological Analysis; Claude Shannon, Information Theory; Alan Turing, Computational Completeness; Benoit Mandelbrot, Fractals; John Nash, Game Theory; Richard Bandler, Neuro-Linguistic Programming (NLP); all my associates at Apple and everyone else who contributed to Agile; and the entire Open Source Community.

2. Why you need Predictive Innovation®

- 100 miles-per-gallon
- 5-star crash test equivalency
- $25,000 sales price
- 0 – 60 in less than 5 seconds
- 149 miles-per-hour top speed
- Cargo room fits 20 bags of groceries

**Designed and built by
an international team
of volunteers
<u>in just 3 months</u>**

Your competition is global, constantly improving, and can always undercut your price. You must innovate to survive.

Cheap foreign labor is not your biggest threat. Automation and user collaboration are dropping prices below cheap all the way to free. Can you compete with free?

If you use old methods you will fail. Even if you copy their methods you will never catch up. The only way to get ahead and stay ahead is to think and act predictively.

Thomas Edison's trial and error approach died 100 years ago with the horse drawn wagon. Fail-fast, fail often only leads to failure. You have limited time and budget but infinite competition. You need to know what customers will want before they start demanding it. You also need to know the most profitable way to deliver it before you start. Plus, you need to see future challenges and have solutions ready when challenges pop up.

Return on investment is the point of innovation. Regardless of how creative or fashionable a product is, if everyone involved doesn't receive a significant benefit it will fail. That means investors, workers, and customers all must receive enough benefit to get them to be happy with their investment of time and money.

Maximize profits and minimize investment. That means providing the most benefit to the most people while using the least time and materials to do it. You need to know both what to make and how to make it. You also must see the entire market so you don't miss valuable opportunities. Random approaches can't guarantee you collect all the value in the most efficient order. Only a structured system like Predictive Innovation can minimize investment, reduce risk, and maximize reward.

Old Way

The most common approach to innovation is:

1. Brainstorm a lot of creative ideas
2. Filter out bad ideas
3. Launch the product
4. Pray

That process is called Staged Gate. It's used by companies worldwide. Despite over 50 years of improvement, 40% of products launched, fail. Nearly random!

The average Staged Gate process requires 300 ideas to get 1 success[1]. All of that filtering costs a lot of time and money. It costs 9 times more than just launching a single project. That extra expense means that only ideas expected to have huge profits are even considered. The smaller less risky projects are ignored because they won't make up for all of that time and money wasted on filtering.

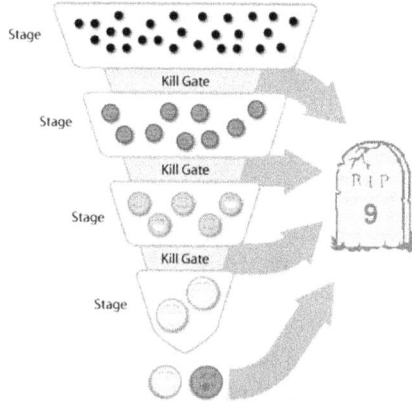

Illustration 1: Staged Gate has 40% Failure Rate at Launch

It also means you need a huge up front investment to start. For small companies that just isn't possible. The smaller company can't risk the failure of trying to innovate so it is guaranteed the failure of competition.

Before you blame Staged Gate, that 40% rate doesn't happen to everyone who uses it.

A study of 576 projects at 360 Fortune 500 companies revealed a dramatic difference in results. (Stevens & Burley 2003) [2]

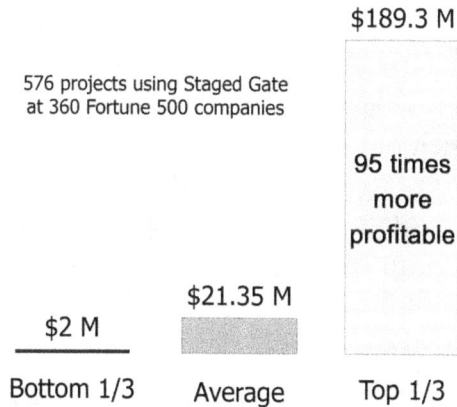

576 projects using Staged Gate at 360 Fortune 500 companies

$189.3 M

95 times more profitable

$21.35 M

$2 M

| Bottom 1/3 | Average | Top 1/3 |

---

1 Stevens, Greg and Burley, James (1997), "3,00 Raw Ideas = 1 Commercial Success", Research Technology Management, 40(3), May-June 1997, 16-27.

2 Stevens, Greg A. and Burley, James (2003) "Piloting the Rocket of Radical Innovation" Research Technology Journal Volume 46 (2): March – April 2003: 16-25

All of the projects use similar Staged Gate processes but the Top 1/3 had a 96% success rate and were 95 times as profitable.

What did the top performers do differently?

There are two types of innovation systems: Thinking Systems and Doing Systems. Staged Gate is a Doing System. It manages risk.

Creativity is:

Common Systems

- Unpredictable
- Unreliable
- Unfocused
- Inefficient
- Emotional
- Person Specific

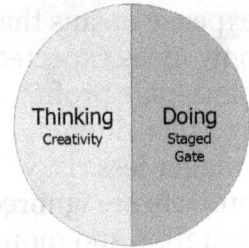

The creativity brainstorming approach to generating ideas causes all of the risk that Staged Gate tries to manage. Replace the Thinking System and all that risk goes away. You can get 96% success and 95 times more profits.

New Approach: Predictive Innovation®

Using Predictive Innovation for your Thinking System turns everything upside down. Instead of starting with a bunch of random ideas, it starts with objective criteria organized into a structure so nothing is overlooked.

Instead of filtering down, you build up. You start with a stable foundation that supports growth of a family of interrelated products.

Predictive Innovation®

Family of Successful Products

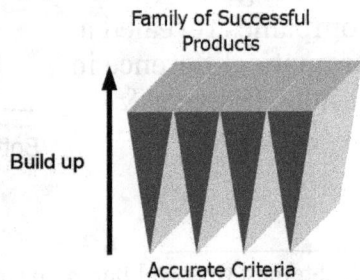

Build up

Accurate Criteria

You multiply profits while reducing risk. All of your work and investment supports future innovation. Profit margins increase over time instead of decrease. And instead of struggling for new ideas it gets easier and easier as you build on your strategy.

Seeing the entire idea space makes the difference.

Studying patents and product literature of thousands of products shows that most products cover less than 1% of their innovation potential and most industries only cover 13%. That leaves over 80% of the idea space unexplored.

Idea Space

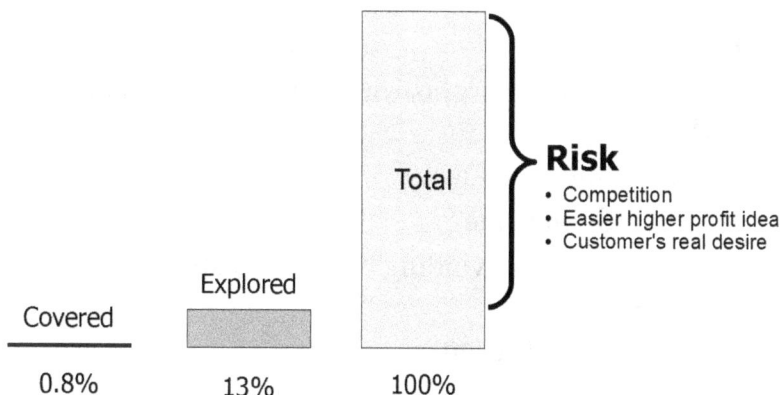

Risk
- Competition
- Easier higher profit idea
- Customer's real desire

Total

Explored

Covered

0.8%   13%   100%

That unexplored idea space is missed opportunity. It's also increased risk from competition or that the easier higher profit idea was never tried. Notice that the ratios of the idea space are nearly identical to the profits of the projects in the Staged Gate study. The Top performers explored more of the idea space resulting in 96% success and 95 times more profits.

Benefits

Increase profits

- See all the ideas customers will want, and ideas they won't
- Start development and launch at the right time
- Make a family of products & services to multiply value
- Build on a core you control

Reduces Risk
- Start earlier while avoiding rushing
- Reduce time to market
- See all the alternatives so you choose the best for you
- Quickly find solutions to technical challenges

Maximizes ROI
- Higher profit margins with the right product at the right time
- Higher success rate
- Find hidden value
- Lower costs by avoiding building costly infrastructure
- Quicker break-even
- More projects by seeing connections between projects

Secures Long Term Value
- Stay ahead of competition
- Use competitors to your advantage
- Block threats with advanced knowledge and having strategies in place to deal with change
- Develop markets you can own
- Quickly respond to events

Ways to use Predictive Innovation

New product development

Finding and developing new products and services is one way to use Predictive Innovation.

Traditional new product development (NPD) and even Agile/Lean approaches tend to require:

- Different design for each product generation.

- Different manufacturing processes for each product generation.
- Expensive and time-consuming launches for each new product generation.
- Difficulty standardizing components & supplies.

Using Predictive Innovation for new product development (NPD) turns all of that around, it enables:

- one design for multiple products & multiple generations of a product thus multiplying return on investment
- one manufacturing process for multiple products and generations, with easy switching from one to another thus multiplying productivity
- efficient standardization of components and supplies thus simplifying processes and reducing overhead & startup costs.

Process improvement

Improving your processes helps you gain an advantage even if you are selling a commodity product. Internal innovations are one of the most valuable ways to use Predictive Innovation.

Business strategy

Strategy turns a good idea into a successful business. The full spectrum view only available with Predictive Innovation gives you the advantage of the most successful strategies.

Marketing

Knowing how to communicate with customers is just as important as having what they want. Predictive Innovation gives you a structured approach to understand and translate fuzzy desires into objective results you can measure.

Intellectual Property

Smart people recognize that intangible assets have become more valuable than tangible assets. Protecting their intellectual property is often a major concern to inventors & business people. However, that isn't your goal. Your real goal is to maximize the value you receive from all available intellectual property. Only Predictive Innovation can do that.

Patents & copyrights are frequently associated with innovation but that is a very incomplete view of the total value. Only a portion of all intellectual property can be patented or copyrighted.

	Patented	Not Patented
Patentable	Your patents	Unclaimed idea space
Non-patentable	Other people's patents	Public domain

As much as 75% of the idea space can't be patented or copyrighted but you still can profit if you know how.

Predictive Innovation increases the value of intellectual property more in ways traditional approaches can't because Predictive Innovation can efficiently describe the entire idea space. Seeing the entire idea space helps you maximize the value of intellectual property, minimize the risk, and neutralize threats.

When you describe the entire idea space you can:
- Build Patent Fences to protect the entire idea space
- Find alternatives to litigation
- Increase the overall value
- Limit damage from infringement
- Discourage litigation from patent trolls
- Avoid conflicts in the market place

This is just a sampling of the ways Predictive Innovation helps with intellectual property.

Investment decision making

Predictive Innovation is the only way to measure the true value of ideas before spending time or money on development.

Calculate the full value and the real risk. See the amount of the entire idea space your investment will buy, not just a share of a market.

Core Skills

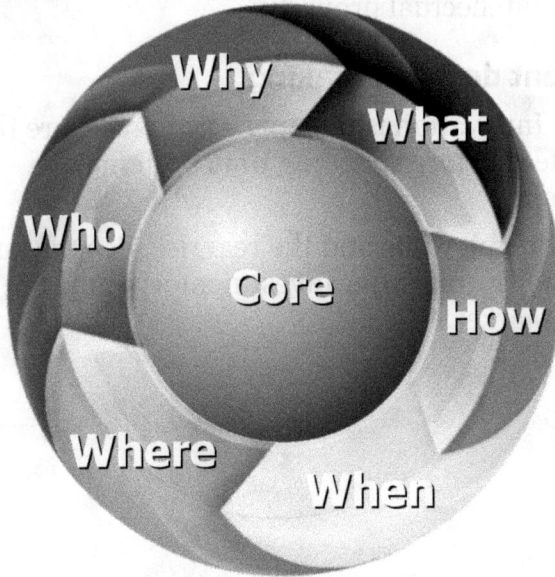

The goal of this book is to provide you with the core skills needed to start using Predictive Innovation. You will learn the basics that apply to everything else you will do with Predictive Innovation.

There are six key pieces of knowledge provided by Predictive Innovation: *What* customers want; *How* to make it; *When* to make and release it; *Why* customers want it; *Who* uses, buys and makes it; and *Where* to focus on.

What

The most important part of innovation is knowing what customers want. Predictive Innovation shows you in advance what customers will want so that you are always two steps ahead. *What* isn't just the basic idea but the precise requirements needed to satisfy both customers and providers of innovations. Knowing what to make in advance also makes it possible to create business strategies that neutralize competition. You are in control.

How

A good idea isn't good if you can't profitably deliver it. Predictive Innovation shows you how to solve technical challenges. You eliminate barriers to develop and deliver products, services and strategies.

You are prepared with inexpensive easy-to-do responses to even unexpected changes. That keeps you focused on profitably satisfying customers" unmet desires.

When

Predicting the right time to start developing and the right time to release a new product is a key value of Predictive Innovation®. Starting too soon will lead to wasted effort and money and starting too late increases risk of competition and reduced profit margins. Predictive Innovation will help you create a step-by-step strategy to deliver exactly the right product at exactly the right time to maximize profits and minimize risk.

Where

Where is more than a geographic location. *Where* is about relationships. *Where* in your organization or process to focus efforts to improve? *Where* are your products in the progression of innovation towards the ideal? *Where* helps you measure your success, how far yet to achieve, and pinpoint the best use of your resources.

Who

Who are your potential customers? *Who* will make it? *Who* will invest? Innovations satisfy desires of people. Understanding *Who* is crucial to successful innovation.

Finding new customers for existing products is the highest profit, lowest risk way of innovating. Predictive Innovation® will guide you in finding all the potential markets for your existing and new products. This helps you achieve your goals faster and easier.

Who will make the product or deliver the service? Doing everything under one roof is not the only way to deliver a product. Finding the best combination of in-house, outsourced, open-sourced, and un-sourced can be the difference between success and failure. Predictive Innovation® shows you all of the options and how to quickly identify the best combination for you.

Investors want assurance of low risk and large profits. Again there are more investors than the traditional sources. Seeing all sources of investment gets your idea off the drawing board and into customers' hands.

Why

Understanding *Why* customers want a product is essential for creating the most effective communication. Also you need to know *Why* you are making it, *Why* investors will support it. To communicate most effectively you need to speak using the words and feelings they associate with getting *What* they want.

Get Started

Learn the core skills and start thinking predictively.

3. Overview

Anything that can be made or done must be able to be described. If you can't describe it there is no way for you to do it.

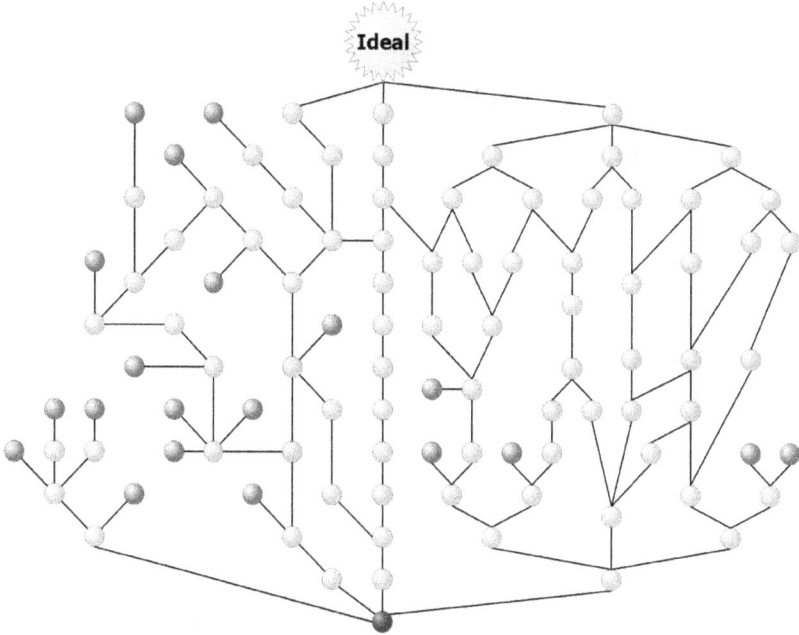

Illustration 2: Paths of Idea Space

Once you describe it, you can also describe the ideal version. The ideal does what you want, when you want, where you want, the way you want, with whom you want, for the price you want with no hassle. If you start from the ideal then go backwards to what is available today, each step is an innovation.

What, How, and Doing it

To innovate you need ideas and to put those ideas into action. Ideas fit into two basic categories: what to make and how to make it. Only when you correctly identify what to make and the most profitable way to make it can you actually make your product or service. Additionally, to accurately measure your performance you need the correct criteria.

This book shows you the basics of how to determine what to make and how to make it. It's up to you to put those ideas into practice.

You need to know what you will make before you can figure out how to make it; but, the ways to make things influences what to make. A pocket MP3 player depends on electricity, which depends on batteries, which depends on the materials to make a battery.

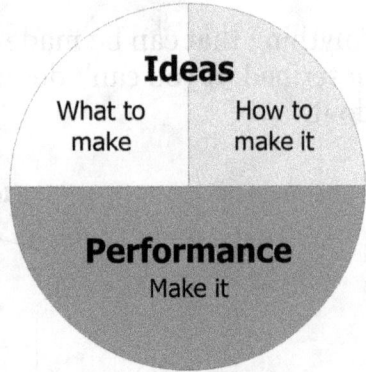

Each step affects the next step. Choices of what to make interact with how to make it. You will use different parts of Predictive Innovation depending on if you are focusing on what or how. You will want to learn all the Core Skills but this table shows which parts to focus on for either What or How.

What	How
• Outcomes	• Dilemmas
• Ideal	• Elements
• 6Ws	• Alternatives
• Satisfaction and Importance Levels	• Functions
• Universal Process	• Components
• Alternatives Progression	• Importance rank order Agile Projects
• Element Combinations	
• Importance 5-point scale	

4. What is Innovation

The word "innovation" is so widely used and misused it has lost some of its meaning. It is essential that you understand what is meant by innovation. This book defines innovation as:

> *"Profitably satisfy an unmet desire"*

The essential words in that definition are <u>satisfy</u> and <u>desire</u>. People have desires. All innovation starts with people. The primary person is the user. What desire does the user have that they want to be satisfied? Understanding users' desires is the crucial first step to innovation.

Inventing does not equal innovating. There are many inventions that don't satisfy an unmet desire. Those inventions might be novel and even do something better than any other way, but if no one desires it done better, the invention will fail as an innovation.

Furthermore, if the product or service never gets to the user it can't satisfy the desire. Unused products don't innovate. Products can fail to get to users because of many reasons including: it's never built, the users never find out about it, or it's too expensive.

Most approaches at innovation focus on creativity and generating ideas. Creative ideas rarely result in innovations. Innovation is not about creative ideas; it's about finding practical solutions that satisfy real people. Innovating is a problem solving activity. Creativity can help in solving problems but you do not need any creativity to innovate. This means innovation is a skill anyone can learn.

For an innovation to make it to users and satisfy their desires it must satisfy the desires of everyone involved in making and delivering it. If the people making and delivering the innovation do not have their desires met, they cannot or will not provide the innovation to users.

People have many desires. When satisfying desires, there are trade-offs. If the trade-off of a solution causes more losses than the value of the desires satisfied, it is not profitable.

To innovate, a solution must cause an overall improvement to all the related desires. That means everyone involved in making, providing, and finally using the innovation must receive more value than it costs or innovating fails.

So when thinking of innovation you must consider the total cost. The total cost is not just the price in dollars but all the desires affected by delivering and using the innovation.

Ideal Product

Users don't care about how their desires are satisfied; they just want their desires satisfied. Users want results. The ideal product does everything you want and nothing you don't. It completely satisfies all the related desires without reducing the satisfaction of any other desire.

> *The ideal product does:*
> *<u>what</u> they want,*
> *<u>when</u> they want,*
> *<u>where</u> they want,*
> *the <u>way</u> they want,*
> *with <u>whom</u> they want,*
> *for the <u>price</u> they want,*
> *with <u>no hassle</u>.*

The ideal is obviously far from what is currently achievable for most products. This ideal gives you a basis to measure existing products and a goal for future products. By describing the ideal product you can step backwards to what is available today and see the path that is needed to reach the future ideal. This is part of the process for predicting innovations.

5. Prerequisites

There are several concepts that are helpful to understand in order to get the most out of Predictive Innovation. This section covers these concepts.

Functional Distinctions

You've probably seen products with long lists of features that don't have much value for the primary function of the product. Some products have differences in the primary function but the differences are so small it doesn't matter. Even large differences that don't relate to the purpose of the product do not mean much to users. The important differences are those that noticeably affect the function. These are Functional Distinctions.

The purpose and the result determine Functional Distinctions. The intended goal of using the product determines which functions it must perform.

For a product that is used by blind people, the color does not matter. However, if the product is used by blind people to show sighted people they are blind, such as a white cane with a red tip, color is very important.

Sometimes the amount causes a Functional Distinction. More or less of the same thing often doesn't have a significant effect but there can be differences of amount that cause a functional difference.

Illustration 3: Thermometer

Water is a requirement of life but if you have too much you can die. Same thing with heat. Too little heat and you freeze to death, too hot and you burn. There are many Functional Distinctions of scale in science. Water below 0°C freezes and is a solid. Between 0°C and 100° C water is a liquid. Over 100°C water is a gas. Solids, liquids, and gasses each have very different properties and function differently.

5.Prerequisites

When the performance level for an Outcome makes a new task possible this is a Functional Distinction. For instance, gasoline engines made the power to weight ratio large enough to make heavier than air flight possible. The basic physics of flight were understood and steam engines had been used to move very large amounts of cargo at high speed for decades before airplanes were built. The reason for this was a Functional Distinction

Illustration 4: Wright Brother's First Flight

between steam engines and gasoline engines. Sometimes Functional Distinctions can be achieved with incremental improvements but usually a paradigm change is required. Steam engines that boil water and exhaust steam will never have the power to weight ratio needed for heavier than air flight because of the massive amount of water needed. The fundamental change of not needing water made heavier than air flight possible.

Illustration 5: Microprocessor

Microprocessors have remained fundamentally the same for the past 50 years. Improvements have been made by incrementally increasing the number of transistors and clock speeds of the chips. When the processing power became enough to handle 16 bits at 44,000

Illustration 6: Compact Disc

per second it was possible to play digitally recorded audio. This made audio CD's possible. And when the speed increased more, video became feasible. These were incremental improvements that caused Functional Distinctions.

Another important Functional Distinction comes from lowering the price enough to reach new markets. There are many ways of lowering the prices including: better production techniques, removing unneeded features, and reducing unneeded levels of performance. All of these make it possible for someone to do something they could not do before because it was too expensive.

Identifying Functional distinctions is the key to finding break-through innovations. Functional distinctions can be identified by: looking at key levels, categorizing features with the Alternative Grid, focusing on different Outcomes, or using a different Element to achieve the result.

Example: Apples & Oranges

What ways are apples different from oranges?

- Color
- Shape
- Skin
- Texture of inside
- Acidity

What ways are apples similar to oranges?

- Fruit
- Grow on trees
- Skin
- Size
- Both will float

What purposes are impacted by the similarities and differences?

- Preventing scurvy
- Making a pie
- Throwing
- Transporting
- Making juice
- Sharing with a friend

Multidimensional Thinking

The word "dimensions" is frequently used in science fiction or by religious gurus. That tends to make a simple subject seem complicated. Also, many of the ways dimensions are taught in math classes are too abstract for most people to see how or why to think in multiple dimensions. The truth is, we constantly think in multiple dimensions.

An example of dimensions is the different aspects of paper. Some ways to describe paper are rule, texture, color, and material. Each of those aspects are functionally distinct dimensions. You can visualize those 4 dimensions of paper with a grid.

Illustration 7: Ruled paper

Paper Idea Space		Smooth			Matte		
		Wood	Rice	Hemp	Wood	Rice	Hemp
Lined	White						
	Yellow						
	Pink						
Plain	White						
	Yellow						
	Pink						
Graph	White						
	Yellow						
	Pink						

This grid describes a portion of the idea space of paper. Just like a 2-dimensional map provides coordinates for a physical location, there are coordinates in the idea grid. A geographic map uses longitude and latitude. The map of the paper idea space uses rule, color, texture, and material.

This map of the paper idea space does not cover the entire idea space of paper. It is missing some dimensions such as size, shape, thickness, etc. Additionally the grid does not show the full range for the dimensions listed. There are more colors than white, yellow, and pink. There are more textures than smooth and matte.

Complexity and Fractals

You've probably seen pictures of fractals. Images of fractals have been popular ever since Benoît Mandelbrot coined the phrase in 1975 to describe these amazing complex shapes created by simple rules.

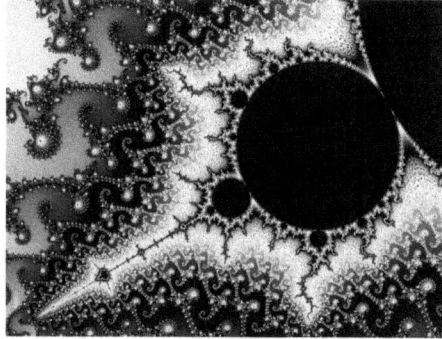
Illustration 8: Mandelbrot Set

The mathematically interesting thing about fractals is that very simple rules, endlessly repeated, create tremendously complex yet orderly shapes. If you zoom in to a fractal you discover that the complex branching shapes are repeated infinitely.

The complexity comes from the results of the previous step being used in the next step. This is exactly what happens with innovation. Choices in the past affect the choices in the now, which affect choices in the future.

Time

There are three functionally distinct ways to look at time. The first is Point-time. When you set an appointment for 9 am Monday that is a point in time.

The other way to look at time is Time-span. If you say something took 4-hours or 17-days that is a span of time.

The third way to think of time is Event-time. When something happens. You don't know the day, minute, or hour until it happens. You are watching for the event to occur.

Logic

There are a few essential elements of logic you need to use Predictive Innovation. You must grasp the concept of Cause and Effect and understand the two logical fallacies: Post Hoc, and Cum Hoc.

Reviewing predicate logic will also help. There are many free resources online to help you review logic.

Standard Units of Measure

There are seven standard physical units of measure. All other physical units of measure are combinations of these seven.

Standard Physical Base Units http://www.bipm.org/en/si/base_units/		
Unit	**Abbreviation**	**Property**
meter	m	distance
kilogram	kg	mass
second	s	time
ampere	A	electric current
kelvin	K	temperature
mole	mol	amount of substance
candela	cd	intensity of light

Length and width are distances so they are measured in meters. Area is length times width so it is measured in meter times meters or square meters.

Speed is distance traveled per unit of time. It is measured in meters per second, m/s.

Length

Width

Practice breaking things down into the physical base units to help you see conceptional base units. This is a key part of Predictive Innovation.

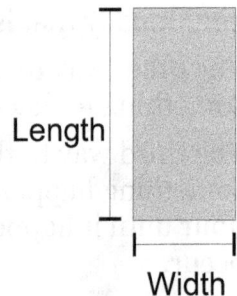

Exercise

1. List ways gold is the same as wood.

2. List ways gold is different from wood.

3. List purposes affected by the ways gold and wood are different.

4. List purposes affected by the ways gold and wood are the same.

5. List purposes not affected by the differences of gold and wood.

6. List purposes not affected by the ways gold and wood are the same.

7. List units to measure gold.

8. List units to measure wood.

6. Dimensions of Predictive Innovation

There are 6 dimensions used in Predictive Innovation. Finding What, How, When, and Where primarily deal with 3 of these dimensions. Why and Who requires more depth of all 6 dimensions. The 6 dimensions are:

Actors

Scenarios

Alternatives

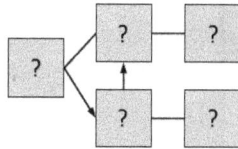

Outcomes

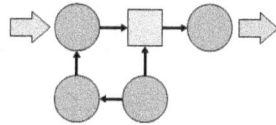

Elements

1. Actors – are people involved in making and using innovations
2. Desires – are the focus of innovation
3. Scenarios – are the boundaries of a set of desires
4. Alternatives – the ways of satisfying desires
5. Outcomes – are the objective criteria that defines satisfaction
6. Elements – are the detailed parts of an Outcome

Actors

Actors

There are 8 types of Actors. Each Actor can be a single person or multiple people. There is always at least one person who is the User. Users are the central focus of innovation. If the users' desires are not satisfied innovation fails. The 8 types of Actors are:

Customer	User
	Beneficiary
	Decider
	Payer
Provider	Designer
	Builder
	Seller
	Communicator

Customers are divided into four distinct roles: Beneficiary, User, Buyer, and Payer. Roles can be performed by one or more people but someone performs each of the roles. The desires of the person acting in that role are different from the desires related to the other roles.

Users are people who use the product or service. There must be at least one User. Satisfying the desires of the User is essential to innovation. Examples of Users' desires are:

- How well the product performs the task
- Feelings related to using the product.

Beneficiaries experience the benefits of the product or service. In most cases the User and the Beneficiary are the same person but not always. Products used in performing a service have a different User than the Beneficiary.

Deciders make the decision to purchase the product or service. Examples of Deciders' desires are:

- price
- warranty
- where to purchase the product

Payers supply the money or materials for the innovation. For consumer products the User, Buyer and Payer are often the same person. In business these are usually three different people. Examples of Payers' desires are:

- Return on Investment
- Total cost
- Achieving a larger strategy

Provider is divided into four roles:

- designer
- builder
- seller
- communicator

Provider can be divided differently but these four provide a sufficiently accurate description to understand the process. Just like customers these could be a single person or multiple people. The provider could also be the same person as the customer and each of the roles could be shared by people acting in other roles. So the User could be Builder and the other 6 roles be someone else.

Designers convert desires into actionable designs. This frequently is more than one person. Examples of Designers' desires are:

- Know criteria to satisfy desires of Actors
- Access to technology
- Interesting challenge

Builders convert design into real products. For services the builder does the work. Builders are often many different people. Examples of Builders' desires are:

- Ease of production
- Tools needed
- Start up costs

Sellers deliver the product or service to the User. The Seller is involved in the purchase transaction. Examples of Sellers' desires are:

- Size of market
- Quantity discounts
- Turn over
- Profit margins
- Hassles of delivering products or services

Communicator gathers information and translates between Actors. Examples of Communicators' desires are:

- Know the desires of Actors
- Able to reach other Actors
- Accuracy of communication

Customers act as more than just Users. There are markets and innovations for each Actor in a Scenario. Innovation starts by satisfying Users.

Desires

Profitably satisfying unmet desires is the definition of innovation. All Actors have desires. To innovate everyone involved must have their desires satisfied.

Desires alone are not helpful for innovation because desires are subjective and fluctuate. To effectively innovate you must convert <u>subjective</u> desires into <u>objective</u> Outcomes.

The first step of innovation is identifying desires for the User then each other Actor.

Scenarios

Desires have a context. Scenarios are the over-all goal. The desires for drinking coffee in the morning at work are very different from drinking coffee at night while on a date.

There are different desires for each Actor in each Scenario. Innovations satisfy the desires for a scenario. Scenarios define the boundaries of desires. Before you can identify desires you must first establish the scenario.

Outcomes

Outcomes are the objective criteria for satisfying desires. Outcomes can be measured or observed. There are approximately 7 Outcomes for each scenario. Before you can start innovating you need to convert the subjective desires into objective Outcomes. The essential Outcomes for a scenario never change. This is one of the keys to predicting innovations.

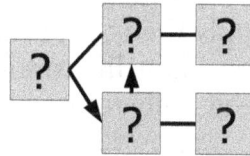

Elements

Each Outcome can be broken down into 7 Elements.
Elements help organize innovation efforts and stimulate
thought.

The 7 Elements are:

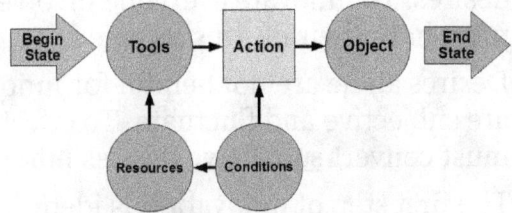

Illustration 9: Elements

1. Objects
2. Begin State
3. End State
4. Actions
5. Tools
6. Conditions
7. Resources

There can be many of each Element for each Outcome but
there are always at least one of each Element per Outcome.

Alternatives

Alternatives are one of the
most powerful parts of
Predictive Innovation.
Everything you do in
Predictive Innovation will use
the 15 Alternatives. You can
apply the 15 Alternatives in
your daily life to solve

	+	-	=	→	~
1					
m					
∞					

15 Alternatives Grid Symbols

seemingly impossible problems, to resolve conflicts, to
spark new ideas, and to organize your thoughts.

There are 15 ways to satisfy any desire. The 15 Alternatives
describe all the ways. There are at least one of each of the 15
Alternatives for solving any problem.

For each Element of each Outcome there is at least one
solution approach for each of the 15 Alternatives. This
means there are always at least 105 innovations for any
Scenario. Knowing this is one of the ways Predictive
Innovation helps you maximize profits, minimize risk and
neutralize competition.

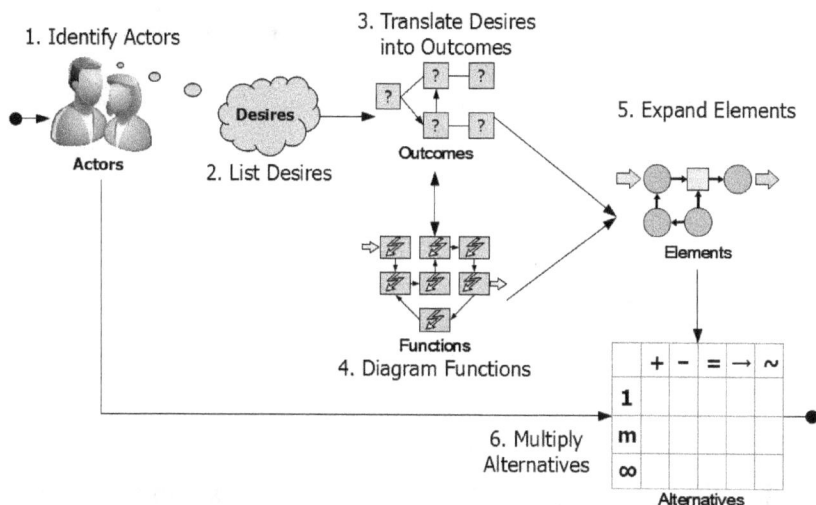

1. Identify Actors

Actors

2. List Desires

3. Translate Desires into Outcomes

Desires

Outcomes

4. Diagram Functions

Functions

5. Expand Elements

Elements

6. Multiply Alternatives

Alternatives

Innovation Process

1. Identify users. What do they want to do that identifies them?

2. Describe the tasks the users are trying to do and the desire it satisfies.

3. Translate desires into Outcomes.

4. Convert Outcomes into Functions

   a) Identify Outcomes for each Function

5. Expand the Elements for each Outcome and Function

   a) Identify all the Objects for each Outcome and Function.

   b) Identify begin and End States of the Objects.

   c) Define the desired End States for each Object.

   d) Find Actions that cause each of the End States.

   e) Describe relevant Conditions for each Action.

   f) List available Resources.

6. Multiply Alternatives

Exercise

Register online for free answer sheets to all exercises

1. List the Actor type for a customer.

2. When is the Beneficiary not the User?

3. Why are Desires not helpful for innovation?

4. What never changes about a Scenario?

5. How many types of Elements form an Outcome?

6. List all of the Elements.

7. How many ways are there to satisfy any desire?

7. Basics of Predictive Innovation

Predictive Innovation makes it possible to accurately understand what customers desire now and in the future and how to overcome technical challenges to satisfying those desires. In this way it merges marketing, engineering and business strategy. The key is how it breaks down systems into easy to manage dimensions. All innovation and problem solving uses three specific dimensions:

- Outcomes
- 7-Elements
- 15-Alternatives

By using these three specific dimensions, all the innovations for any product or service can be accurately described even if current technology can't build it.

Physical objects can be described using height, width, and depth. Similarly, systems can be described using the three dimensions: Outcomes, 7-Elements, and 15-Alternatives.

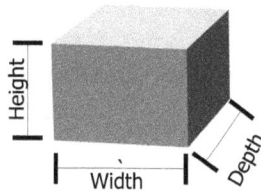

Outcomes

Outcome is the result of something happening. For Predictive Innovation we use a broader and more formal meaning.

> *Outcome is an observable state resulting from a cause.*

Speed, color, or temperature are observable States. A State can also be an event that did or did not happen. The State of any Outcome is classified into one of three categories:

- desired
- undesired
- neutral

Most systems can be described using between 5 and 9 Outcomes. If a system is complex it might require dividing the system into smaller sub-systems to be manageable.

When each of the Outcomes of a system are in the desired State the overall goal is achieved.

Predictive Innovation uses Outcome Diagrams to graphically represent the systems for satisfying people's desires. Outcome diagrams are a type of flow chart. Instead of showing steps in a process it displays all the conditions or "if" statements to achieve the overall goal. In words an Outcome diagram says:

> If A and B and C Then my desires are
> satisfied for this Scenario.

7-Elements

Predictive Innovation considers more than the End State, it looks at all of the Elements of the Outcome. Each Outcome is made up of 7 types of Elements. These Elements are :

- Objects
- Begin States
- End States
- Actions
- Tools
- Conditions
- Resources

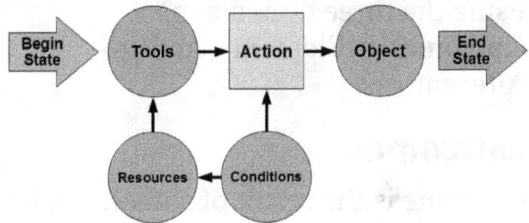

The 7 Elements of an Outcome can be visualized in a diagram. You can see the relationship of Elements. You can see that the Begin States are processed to produce the End States. Tools, Conditions, and Resources affect the Action performed on or by the Object.

Object is the focus of the Outcome, it is what has the State. Look for nouns in descriptions of desires to find Objects.

Begin States are the relevant State for the Outcome being considered. The Begin State can be desired, undesired, or neutral. You want to keep desired States and change undesired States into desired States. If you can't achieve a desired State you might accept a neutral State based on the States of other Outcomes.

End States are the State after the Action has occurred. The End State is the result of the Action. Again End States can be desired, undesired or neutral.

Actions cause the Begin State of the Object to become an End State. Action causes a State to change or remain the same. Actions are verbs.

Tools are something directly used in the Action. Something becomes a Tool based on how it is used.

Conditions are all the other States that influence the Action affecting the result. For instance, the temperature of paint influences how well it sticks to a surface. The texture of a surface is another Condition that affects how well paint sticks.

Resources are anything available in the environment that can be used to perform the Action. The temperature of a room could be intentionally used to speed or slow the process of painting. Resources can be physical or information. Knowing the temperature can help in performing the Action of painting.

Each Outcome can have many different Elements for each of the 7-Element types. There can be many different Objects, Begin State, End State, Actions, Tools, Conditions, and Resources. Every Outcome has at least one of each of the 7-Element types.

15-Alternatives

The 15-Alternatives is one of the unique discoveries of Predictive Innovation. There are 15-Alternative types for achieving any task.

	Direct	Indirect	Stable	Make Stable	Return to Stable
Single					
Multiple					
Continuous					

15 Alternatives Grid

The 15 Alternatives fit into a 3 by 5 grid. The rows are Single (1), Multiple (m), and Continuous (∞). The three rows represent Scales. The columns are Direct (+), Indirect (-), Stable (=), Make Stable (→), and Return to Stable (~). The columns represent Directions. These combine to describe all 15 ways of accomplishing a goal.

We often abbreviate the rows and columns of the Alternatives Grid with symbols. Aside from being abbreviations, these symbols can be helpful for understanding combinations that can be defined with the 15 Alternatives.

	+	-	=	→	~
1					
m					
∞					

15 Alternatives Grid Symbols

All of your Predictive Innovation work will involve understanding, identifying and using Outcomes, Elements, and Alternatives.

8. Alternatives

	Direct +	Indirect -	Stable =	Make Stable →	Return to Stable ~
Single 1					
Multiple M					
Continuous ∞					

15 Alternatives Grid

The Alternatives Grid describes every possible way to satisfy a single Condition.

Each box in the grid represents a general way or approach to achieving a goal or result. Five columns and three rows means there are at least 15 ways to achieve any goal.

Each box in the Alternatives Grid is a general description. It describes a type of Alternative. There can be many examples of each type. All the possible Alternatives can be categorized into one of the 15 types.

The 15 Alternatives describe all the possible ways to achieve a goal because they are all the basic approaches.

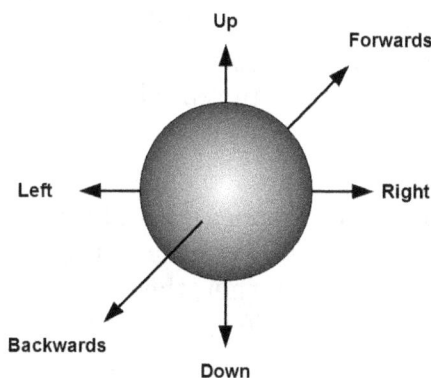

To understand how you can describe every possible combination think about giving directions to go somewhere. If you give someone directions you can break all the steps into six basic movements: up, down, left, right, forwards and backwards.

By combining the six basic movements, you can travel anywhere. The same concept works for Alternatives. The 15 Alternatives describe every possible type of Alternative. It's a framework for solving every problem.

Just because there are 15 types doesn't mean that is the limit. Each box only describes a general type. There could be lots of individual ways that fit in each box. There could be many Continuous Stable Alternatives or Many Single Direct Alternatives.

The boxes of the Alternatives Grid describe every way. This helps you find the ways you can use. Knowing there are at least 15 Alternatives helps you find really good solutions.

If you can't think of something for a box then there's a solution you overlooked. Sometimes one of the Alternatives isn't possible using current technology. You can still describe the basics of how it will work and watch for the technology to become available.

Ways to Use the Alternatives Grid

There are three main ways to use the Alternatives Grid.

1. Find a good Alternative
2. Find all the Alternatives
3. Find an untapped innovation

Sometimes you just want to get something done. When any good Alternative will satisfy your criteria we call that problem solving or solution finding. The way you were trying wasn't working; so, you need a different choice. Use the Alternatives Grid to find an option you like.

When solution finding you don't need to look at every Alternative. Just because there are 15 boxes doesn't mean you must find something for every box. If you find a really good Alternative, use it. If you need another, the Alternatives Grid is always there to guide you to more options.

When making a plan you might want to make sure you have the best choice and Alternatives in case you need to change your plan. The Alternatives Grid is a great tool for planning. Use it to find the best choice. Because it describes all the possible Alternatives, it helps you make sure to consider every option.

If any of the boxes in the Alternatives Grid is empty there is definitely something you missed. This could be a breakthrough waiting to happen. Since you have described what the box must contain you have the upper hand in finding it first.

Scales

	+	-	=	→	~
1					
m					
∞					

The 3 rows of the Alternatives Grid are called Scales. The three Scales are: Single, Multiple, and Continuous. We use the symbols 1, M, and either ∞ or C to represent the scales.

Each of the three scales are functionally distinct[3] from each other. Having only one of something is very different from having more than one. Doing something in one step is often very different from breaking it up into multiple steps. You can't step over a hole in two steps. You either step over it in one step or fall in. One is functionally distinct from multiple and continuous.

Most things fit in the many or multiple scale. Once you have a quantity of something there isn't a Functional Distinction between a small amount or a large amount. The big difference happens when you have all of something.

Having all of something is very different than having many. One type of continuous is all. When you have all of something you can do things that are not possible when you have many or even most of it. Having all of something is different from many and it is different from having the one and only. Continuous also means no divisions or breaks, it's

---

3   See Prerequisites section for more explanation of Functional Distinction

smooth. Continuous is the difference between a digital gauge and a dial with a needle.

Breaking things into these categories helps you think about how they function, and what can be done. These Functional Distinctions are important for finding solutions.

Single

	+	-	=	→	~
1					
m					
∞					

There is a Single Alternative for each of the directions. Words used to describe Single are: single, one, once, only, exclusive, or unique.

Apply Single to: who, what, why, where, when, and with.

Single Element: Object, Begin State, End State, Action, Tool, Condition, Resource

Think of a Single: person, purpose, place, use, time, piece, or step.

Disposable plastic eating utensils are Single use. These are also a Single piece and made from a Single material. Each of these have a Single purpose.

Illustration 10: Single use, disposable

Custom made items are one of a kind. These items are exclusive. When used to make an item unique, Single can increase value.

Illustration 11: One of a kind shoes

Illustration 12: Elastic waistband, one piece shorts

The elastic band in the waist hold up one pair of shorts. The shorts are one-piece.

The Ford Model T came in one color, black, to simplify manufacturing and reduce cost.

Illustration 13: Ford Model T One Color

Multiple

	+	-	=	→	~
1					
m					
∞					

Multiple or many is more than one. Multiple provides flexibility with limits, choices with structure.

Multiple items usually have quantities you can count. Multiple can be many of the same item or many related items. Many can also mean parts. So instead of a single piece it has many pieces or many steps to perform a task.

Multiple applies to who, what, why, where, when, and with.

Think of multiple choice, pieces, steps, customers, locations, prices, or models.

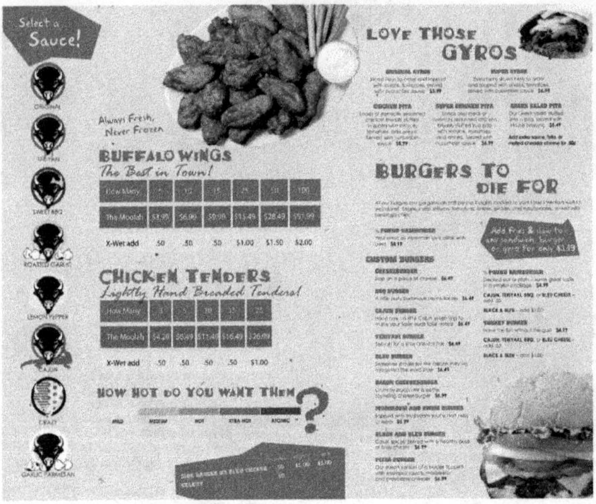

Illustration 14: Menu

Menus provide multiple choices. There are options with limits. There is flexibility but structure.

Multiple colors of cars are offered by manufacturers. This provides variety without complexity.

Illustration 15: Cars in multiple colors

Most cars have options for different components. This allows flexibility for customers but control for manufacturers. Cars carry multiple passengers.

Illustration 16: Belts are used on multiple pants

A belt can be worn with many different pairs of pants.

A reversible belt is more than one color.

Adjustable sizes fit many waists.

Continuous

Continuous is the extreme in any direction, not just more but the most possible.

	+	-	=	→	∼
1					
m					
∞					

Continuous items are measured by volume or weight if they are measured at all. Words used to describe continuous are:

- all
- any
- every
- none

- always
- forever
- whenever
- never

- everyone
- anyone
- whoever
- no one

Continuous applies to who, what, where, when, why, and with. All 7 Elements of an Outcome apply to continuous. Continuous Scale is similar to Stable Direction

An all-you-can-eat buffet has many examples of continuous.

- All you can eat
- No waiting
- No servers
- Anything on the menu.

Illustration 17: All You Can Eat Buffet

Illustration 18: Skype, free chat, voice and video conferencing

Skype provides free chat, voice and video conferences between users and unlimited long distance phone calls for a fixed price.

Restroom is accessible to anyone. The sign can be read by people who can see and cannot. Unisex so anyone can use it.

Illustration 19: Handicap Unisex Bathroom

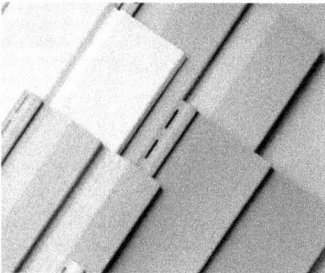

Illustration 20: Vinyl siding, never paint

The color of vinyl siding is forever. You never need to paint it.

Custom made items allow you to have anything. If the product is information, like the design on the T-Shirt, you can make unlimited copies.

Your Image Here

Illustration 21: Custom made T-Shirt

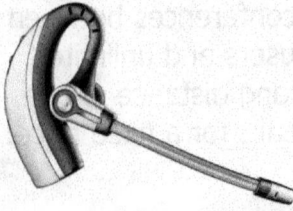

Wireless headset has no wires and requires no hands to use. If it is used with a mobile phone it can be taken anywhere. A headset allows you to talk while driving so it's anytime.

Illustration 22: Wireless headset

A tattoo is an example of continuous in several ways. It is permanent, always, and forever.

Illustration 23: Tattoo , always, forever

Directions

The 5 columns of the Alternatives Grid are called Directions. The five directions are: Direct, Indirect, Keep Stable, Make Stable, and Return to

	+	-	=	→	~
1					
m					
∞					

Stable. Like the 3 scales the 5 Directions are functionally distinct from each other.

The symbols we use for the Directions only hint at the true functionality of each Direction. The first three, Direct +, Indirect -, and Stable = cover the ideas of more, less, and same. More, less, and same are obviously functionally distinct from each other. Makes Stable → and Return to Stable ~ are functionally distinct versions of Stable.

Understanding the differences of the Directions involves learning an aspect of multidimensional thinking. When thinking in only one dimension we have opposites of each other such as more and less, + and -. Clearly more and less are opposites of each other. But stable, =, is the opposite of change. So Stable, =, is the opposite of both more +, and less -.

Stable can also be thought of as zero (0). If you add or subtract zero from anything it does not change. You can achieve a stable position by making a change or by undoing a change. In that way the change is zero.

Makes Stable starts at a State then ends in the final Stable State. Return to Stable starts at a State then changes and finally returns to the original State. Most often we think of the initial State as being the desired State but it could be any State.

Each of the 15 Alternatives apply to all of the 7 Elements. It's also helpful to think of the 6 Ws: Who, What, Where, Why, When, and With. Who uses it, buys it, decides to use it, and wants it? What is it being done by or to? Where is it being done? When is it being done? With which products, people, or processes is it being used? Why use it? Why is how to decide the Alternative to use.

Direct

	+	-	=	→	~
1					
m					
∞					

It directly satisfies the condition. You can also think of direct as positive such as doing something versus not doing something. Also think of add, increase, or more. If the Direct Function is stopped the desired condition stops.

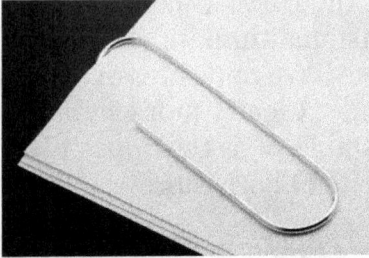

Paper clips directly hold the paper together. If it is removed the pieces come apart. Also a paper clips is adding something.

Illustration 24: Paper Clip Directly Holds Paper

Heater directly makes you warm. It adds heat.

Illustration 25: Heater directly warms

Indirect

Indirect is just what it seems like. It's the opposite of the direct approach. Think words such as remove, decrease, and other.

	+	-	=	→	~
1					
m					
∞					

Indirect is very flexible. The direct approach makes the goal happen when you use it. Indirect could make it happen by not doing something. Or it could take the goal away by doing something.

But indirect doesn't apply just to Actions. It could apply to things you use. For instance you want paint that sticks to a surface better. Instead of looking at the paint, look at the surface. Maybe you can do something to the surface to make the paint stick better. Or to the brush or to the room you are painting in.

A very powerful use of Indirect is to check your goal. Some times we state our goal in a way that is limiting. An example is The Food and Drug Administration (FDA) is responsible for "preventing bad medicine from being sold". That sounds like a good goal but is that really what you want?

Isn't the real goal to promote good medicine? If you set up your Alternatives Grid to "promote good medicine" you suddenly have 12 boxes full of good medicine instead of trying to stop bad medicines. See how that could be much more productive?

But sometimes you could use the indirect goal for another purpose. If you were looking for ways to heat food the indirect is to make it cold. Can you see value in making food cold?

Look for all indirect Alternatives including:

- Objects
- Actions
- Resources
- Begin State
- Tools
- End State
- Conditions

Instead of using toxic chemicals to repel bugs, attract them to a bug zapper.

Illustration 26: Attract bugs to zapper instead of repelling with chemicals

Instead of drying dishes, make water not stick.

Illustration 27: Make water not stick

Instead of stopping junk mail, get more then use it as free fuel.

Illustration 28: Junk mail fuel

Illustration 29: Cage keeps tigers out

Illustration 30: Cage keeps tiger in

Both cages protect the people from tigers. Each has different benefits.

Stable

Keep the desired condition. If you start with what you want you want to keep it. Ways to keep the desired goal fit the description of Stable.

	+	-	=	→	~
1					
m					
∞					

Stable options are described with words such as:

- prevent
- hold
- keep
- protect

- store
- save
- avoid
- secure

- ensure
- restrict
- lock
- maintain

The Stable Alternative can apply to all 7 Elements.

- Actions, keep happening or prevent it from happening. Do the same Action.
- Object, keep it's shape, color, size, location, or any other characteristic. Objects can be who as well as what. Apply stable Alternative to Person, who it's happening to, for, with or by and remember preventing for person as well.
- Begin State, start from the same State each time.
- End State, keep the same State, prevent the State from changing
- Tool, holds, protects, restricts, locks, etc. Tool does not change, move, or break.
- Conditions, hold conditions stable, same conditions used each time, etc.
- Resources, use a Resource that is consistent such as gravity.

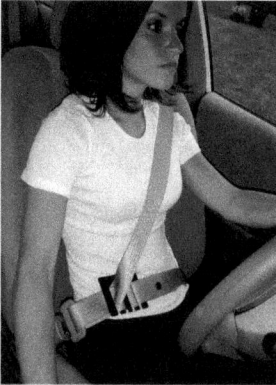

Illustration 31: Seat belt keeps passenger safe

Seat Belt

- Hold person in seat
- Keep person safe
- Prevents serious injury

Sippy Cup

- Lid keeps liquid in
- Avoids spills
- Plastic, prevents breaking

Illustration 32: Sippy cup

Make Stable

	+	-	=	→	~
1					
m					
∞					

Starting from some undesired State it creates a stable desired State. Change a property of an element to bring it to a stable State.

Make Stable options are described with words such as:

- become
- approach
- replace
- result
- reach
- asymptotic

The Make Stable Alternative applies to all 7 Elements.

- Actions, starts with another Action and ends with the appropriate Action.

- Object, becomes the shape, color, size, location, or any other characteristic. Objects can be who as well as what. Apply make stable Alternative to Person, who it's happening to, for, with or by and remember preventing for person as well.

- Begin State, the Begin State changes over time. A system might need to handle many variations until the more efficient supply is established.

- End State, a system that can start with many different start States and results in the same End State.

- Tool, a Tool might form fit to the task or the user.

- Conditions, Condition becomes stable over time.

- Resources, a Resource that accumulates, stabilizes, or becomes available over time. Waste material that is used for padding or sound insulation could be a Make Stable Resource.

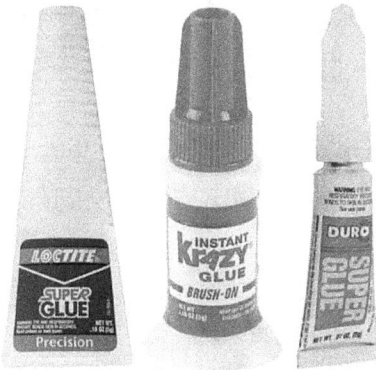

Glue makes things stick together permanently.

Illustration 33: Glue makes stables

Vaccine causes immunity to disease.

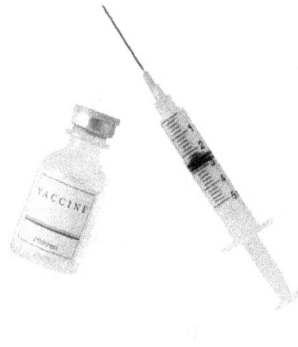

Illustration 34: Vaccine

Fossils happen when water with minerals soaks into the object then the water dries and the object decays away the minerals are left behind as a fossil.

Illustration 35: Fossil, make stable

Return to Stable

Bring the desired State back if it
changes. Like all stable Alternatives
you might have used a direct or
indirect to reach the desired State.

	+	-	=	→	~
1					
m					
∞					

Return to Stable options are described with words such as:

- change
- recover
- restore
- fluctuate
- heal
- recycle
- flexible
- repair
- reuse

Return to Stable Alternative applies to all 7 Elements.

- Actions, change from one Action to another then back
- Object, recovers shape, color, size, location, or any other characteristic. Objects can be who as well as what. Apply make return to stable Alternative to Person, who it's happening to, for, with or by and remember preventing for person as well.
- Begin State, system handles fluctuating Begin State.
- End State, a range of End States.
- Tool, a Tool might adjust to Conditions.
- Conditions, fluctuates.
- Resources, reuse, recycle, restore.

Springs
- Bend and return
- Stretch and return

Illustration 36: Springs

Generator returns power if it fails.

Illustration 37: Generator

Thermostat turns on heat if it gets too cold or air conditioning if it gets too hot. Returns temperature to the desired setting.

Illustration 38: Thermostat

Time and Alternatives

Innovation is always dealing with change so the passage of time is a fundamental concept for innovation. Time is specifically referenced in the directions, especially the Stable Alternatives. Keep Stable, Make Stable and Return to Stable focus on changes in relation to time. Direct and Indirect are less concerned with time and focus on now. Direct Alternatives achieve the goal when the Action is performed and stop when the Action stops. Indirect is the opposite or different from Direct so regarding time it might be not now meaning before or after. When Continuous is applied to time it overlaps the three Stable Alternatives. It's helpful to think about how time is considered for each of the directions.

Combining Scales and Directions

By combining the 3 Scales and the 5 Directions you have 15 Alternatives. For an example look at coloring a wall. Walls can be colored in many different ways. The typical approach is paint. The end user of the wall does not care how the wall gets the desired color, only that it is the desired color without any other negative effects.

This is only a sample of each type. In reality there are at least 105 types with multiple variations for each. As you read these samples think of other ways of doing the same type or other types for each Alternative. Space has been left for you to write down your ideas.

Example: Paint Sticks to Surface

	+	-	=	→	~
1	More Increase Once One thing One way	Decrease Other	Same Once One thing the same	Becomes permanent Improves once Single step	Returns Again Changes once
m	Many more Many times Many steps	Many other	Same many ways Same many times	Becomes permanent in many ways Multiple steps	Changes many times
∞	Increase all Increase any Increase none	All other Any other Decrease all Decrease any	Any same All same	All ways becomes permanent	Always returns Always changes

Direct

	+	-	=	→	~
1					
m					
∞					

Single

Make paint stick better to one type of surface. Paint sticks during a Single Condition such as temperature or humidity. Paint sticks after one coat.

Multiple

Make paint stick better to multiple surfaces. Paint sticks during multiple Conditions, such as hot and cold or low and high humidity. Two step process, primer then paint.

Continuous

Paint sticks to any surface. Paint sticks during any Condition.

Indirect

Single

Wall holds paint better. The brush makes the paint stick better.

	+	-	=	→	~
1					
m					
∞					

Multiple

Wall holds multiple types of coloring such as paint or wallpaper.

Continuous

Wall holds any color or type of coloring. No paint, color is projected on the wall.

Keep Stable

	+	-	=	→	~
1					
m					
∞					

Single

Make the wall from a material that is the desired color.

Multiple

Make the wall from a material that is multiple colors. Color appears the same in multiple Conditions, reacts to light.

Continuous

Any color. No color, it is transparent so you can see the desired Object through it. Continuously reacts to Conditions to always appear as desired.

Make Stable

Single

Single treatment makes it stable,
stain. Single color. Ceiling paint
changes color after drying making it
easier to see where you painted.

	+	-	=	→	~
1					
m					
∞					

Multiple

Multiple colors. Multiple types of surfaces, such as interior,
exterior, walls, ceilings, or floors. Multiple treatments to
make it stable. Multiple step process.

Continuous

Treatment permanently colors any surface. Any color stain.
Stains the entire room or Object at once.

Return to Stable

	+	-	=	→	~
1					
m					
∞					

Single
Returns to color once. Film placed on wall allows dirt to be removed once. Scuff mark removed with heat or a chemical applied to wall once.

Multiple
Returns to color multiple times. Multiple layers that can be removed. Covering is thick allowing it to be sanded to remove stains or scuff marks. Easy to wash.

Continuous
Color projected on the surface that automatically adjusts to display the correct color regardless of conditions.

9. Outcomes

Outcomes are the external state Users associate with their internal desires. When the appropriate desired state occurs, the User feels satisfied. An Outcome is the result of something happening. Causing the desired state is the goal of innovation.

> *Outcome is an observable state resulting from a cause.*

Properly identifying Outcomes is essential for innovation. An innovator can't reliably satisfy desires unless the desired States for all the required Outcomes are known. Traditional creativity based approaches to innovation skip this step. Without knowing the goal, the results are random. Even after filtering ideas through a Staged Gate process with 7 Stages the failure rate of new products is 40%, nearly random. The high level of failure for new product development (NPD) is because Outcomes are not properly defined.

Outcomes are observable. Outcomes have States such as speed, color, or temperature that can be observed or measured. The State can also be an event that did or did not happen. Once the Outcome is defined, you don't need to ask the user if it has been achieved. You can observe the result and determine for yourself if the desired State has been met.

Doctors use a thermometer to check a patient's temperature rather than asking them if they think they have a fever. Objective Outcomes make it possible to reliably determine States.

Perception can be wildly inaccurate. Optical illusions demonstrate the unreliability of perception. All the boxes in Illustration 39 are squares of the same size. To most people

Illustration 39: Optical Illusion Shape

it appears that the squares are trapezoids that change in height from left to right.

You can verify that each box is square and the same size by measuring it. The measurement is objective; it does not depend on your perception. You can tell someone else or even a machine how to measure the boxes and get the same result each time.

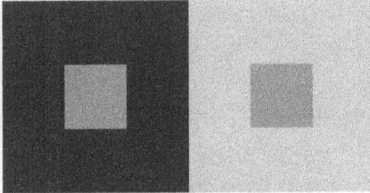

Illustration 40: Optical Illusion Shade

The shade of both the center squares in Illustration 40 are the same. The center square on the right appears darker to most people. The mistaken perception is caused by the tendency for the nervous system to make relative comparisons.

A similar perception error can be created by placing a warm and a cold object near to each other on your skin. The relative difference will mistakenly be perceived as extreme heat. You will feel like your skin is burning even though separately each object is perfectly comfortable to touch.

Optical illusions appear to people with normal functioning vision. When you factor in vision problems like color blindness or astigmatisms, individual perceptions can be drastically different from reality. This is why observable objective Outcomes are so important.

Using objective Outcomes greatly improves the success of innovation projects. Objective Outcomes remove the two most significant causes of random results of new product development. The users subjective fluctuating perception are taken out of the process and communication errors are eliminated. Everyone can work from a consistent well defined set of requirements.

Categories of States

The State of any Outcome is classified into one of three categories:

- desired
- undesired
- neutral

States can be desired, undesired, or neutral in four different ways:

- more
- less
- matches
- does not match

When each of the Outcomes of a scenario are in the desired State the overall goal is achieved. If one Outcome is more important than another, users may accept a neutral State for a less important Outcome as long as the critical Outcome is in the desired State.

You don't need to describe every possible State in detail. All that is important is identifying what makes a State desired, undesired or neutral. For instance, the color red is commonly used for warnings or danger. You don't want to see a red indicator light on a machine turned on. A red light is undesired. Anything else is an acceptable neutral State. Knowing the machine is running properly is a useful feature so it might be green, blue, white, or any color except red to indicate it is on. The "on light" would be a desirable State. No light would be a neutral State.

A comfortable room temperature is 22°C, this is the desirable State. Less than 20°C or more than 25°C are undesirable.[4] Thermostats don't turn on the heat or the air conditioning when the temperature isn't exactly 22°C. There is a neutral range above and below the desired temperature. The temperature is allowed to rise a little

---

4 Metric 20°C, 22°C, and 25°C are approximately 68°F, 72°F, and 77°F

Desired
22ºC

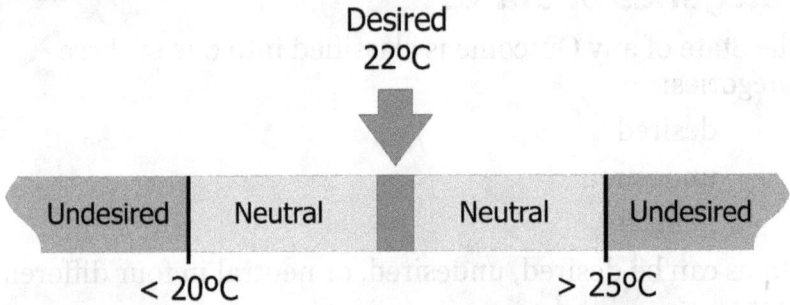

| Undesired | Neutral | | Neutral | Undesired |

< 20ºC   > 25ºC

Illustration 41: Temperatures

above and a little below the desired temperature but prevented from becoming undesired.

Outcome Diagram

The average human can effectively differentiate 7 plus or minus 2 values for a single variable. (Miller, 1956)[5]. This is why phone numbers were originally designed to have 7 digits.

Since the human mind is limited in how many items it can simultaneously focus on, the number of Outcomes needed to satisfy a desire is limited. Most scenarios can be described using between 5 and 9 Outcomes which is 7 plus or minus 2.

Sometimes a Scenario is complex. It might require dividing the scenario into smaller sub-scenarios to be manageable. In most cases you will find that the complexity is a result of scenarios that have been combined and can actually be treated separately.

The fact that people can't effectively pay attention to more than approximately 7 items at once is one of the reasons Predictive Innovation can describe the entire innovation space for a product or service.

All the Outcomes for a scenario can be written as *If...Then* statements.

5   Miller, G. A. (1956). "The magical number seven, plus or minus two: Some limits on our capacity for processing information". Psychological Review 63 (2): 81-97. http://psychclassics.yorku.ca/Miller/

> *If A and B and C Then my desires are satisfied for this Scenario.*

Each of the clauses A, B, and C are Outcomes. When the desired States are achieved for each of the Outcomes, the user's desires for that scenario are satisfied.

Predictive Innovation uses Outcome Diagrams to graphically represent these *If...Then* statements. Outcome Diagrams are a type of flow chart. Instead of showing steps in a process it displays all the conditions or "If" statements to achieve the overall "Then" goal.

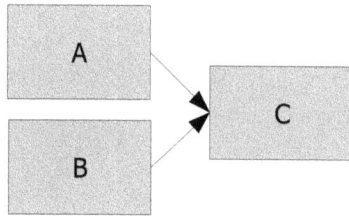

Illustration 42: Outcome Diagram

Outcome Diagrams can show sequential relationships of the different Outcomes. Illustration 42 shows that A and B must occur before C can occur. Outcome Diagrams are essential tools for innovation.

Exercise

1. What are the desired results of using soap?

2. What are some undesired results of using soap?

3. How might you objectively measure the results of using soap?

10.Converting Desires into Outcomes

The core of innovation is satisfying desires. Desires are imprecise, subjective, personal, and frequently change. That makes desires unsuitable to directly use for innovation.

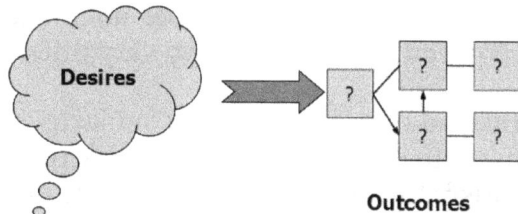

What a person wants changes based on the situation. Time, place, and activity all change the situation. Different people value different things in similar situations. Their desires can be satisfied differently from someone else's desires.

The subjective nature of desires makes it difficult for even customers to express their desires. Not being able to accurately express desires makes it hard for customers to ask for what they want or to explain why a product or service didn't satisfy their desires.

To solve the problem of subjective desires, we convert subjective desires into objective Outcomes. "Customers buy products and services to help them get jobs done." (Ulwick, 2005, p.xvii)[6] Put in the context of performing the job, the subjective desires can be expressed as objective Outcomes. Using the product produces an Outcome. When all the required Outcomes have a desired State, the job is done and the desire is satisfied.

Desires are always in the context of doing some "job". We call that context the Scenario. The required Outcomes for a Scenario always remain the same. Customers can satisfy their desires in very different ways. They can choose different Scenarios to satisfy their desires, however, the

---

6   Ulwick, Anthony (2005). What Customers Want: Using Outcome-Driven Innovation to Create Breakthrough Products and Services. McGraw-Hill ISBN-13: 978-0071408677

Outcomes for each Scenario always remain the same. Some people relax from exercising while others find reading a book relaxing. The fact that a person chooses exercising or reading a book to relax does not change the basic requirements of those two very different activities.

Instead of trying to satisfy subjective desires, we allow the users to choose tasks that satisfy their desires and we satisfy the objective requirements of the task. Desires can be broken down into one or more objective Outcomes by describing the Scenario and each criteria needed to satisfy the desires of that Scenario. Illustration 43: Objective Criteriais a flowchart of how to describe a Scenario and Objective Criteria.

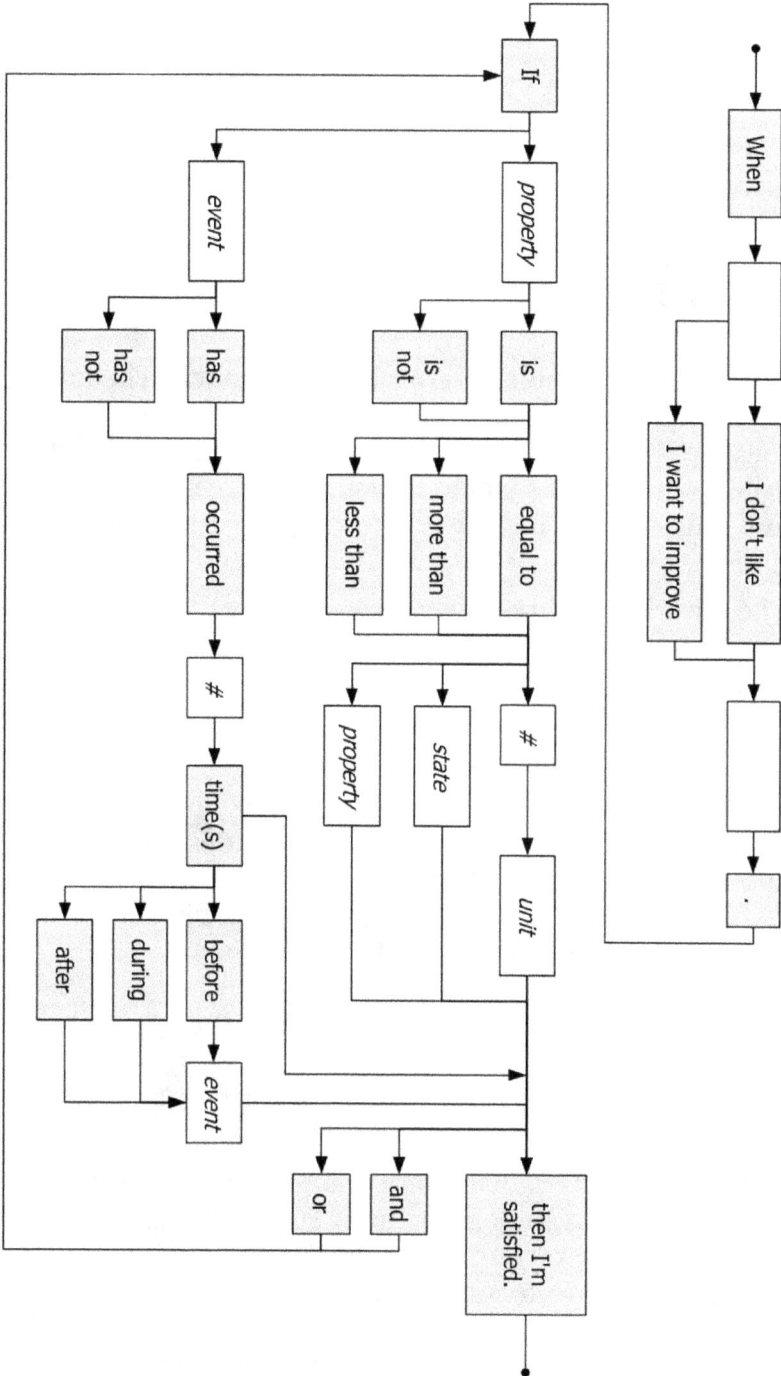

Illustration 43: Objective Criteria

An example of a Scenario is eating sticky peanut butter:

> When eating peanut butter, I don't like
> peanut butter sticking to the roof of my
> mouth.

This describes a specific situation, "eating peanut butter." It also gives a general description of the goal, "not sticking to the roof of my mouth." Now lets write an Objective Outcome for that goal:

> If I lick the roof of my mouth less than 3 licks
> I will be satisfied.

This is an observable and measurable criteria. The number of times the person licks can be observed and you can measure it by counting the number of licks. The objective criteria both allows you to measure the level of satisfaction and it describes exactly what needs to be done to satisfy the desire.

The criteria has three parts.

- Object
- Direction
- State

One way to make peanut butter less sticky is to make it thin like a liquid. Runny peanut butter is not desirable so we should add another criteria.

> When eating peanut butter, I don't like
> peanut butter sticking to the roof of my
> mouth.
> If I lick the roof of my mouth less than 3 licks
> and
> the peanut butter is more than as firm as jelly
> I will be satisfied.

This second criteria has a less scientific unit but it is something that can be measured. The customer might not be able to give exact units but the description is accurate enough for innovators to make a comparison or possibly calculate an actual measurement to use. In this case some measurement of viscosity is likely appropriate but all you need is a consistent criteria that can be observed and reliably communicated.

The stickiness of peanut butter is one aspect of eating peanut butter. The flavor, smell, and visual appearance are other factors that may need to be considered.

The criteria has two parts. The first part broadly but objectively describes the desire, "I don't like peanut butter sticking to the roof of my mouth." The second part is the specific criterion for satisfying the desire. For problem solving you need the specific criterion; however, for innovation work you will mainly use the descriptive portion. This involves restating it in a more generalized form such as:

> The peanut butter must have the correct texture.

When stated this way it is called an Outcome. Outcomes are composed of 7 Elements: Object, Begin States, End States, Actions, Tools, Conditions, and Resources. The Object is the feature that possesses a State that we are trying to optimize. In this example the Object is "texture." The number of licks and the viscosity are States.

Emerging Expectations

Since innovation must satisfy unmet desires it's aiming at a continually moving target. The unmet desires of today will be the bare minimum requirements of tomorrow. Innovation must stay ahead of the desires so you have the time to design, develop, and deliver the innovation at the right moment.

The way to stay ahead is to focus on the criteria several steps ahead of the currently available products. You can do this by imagining the ideal product then looking backwards

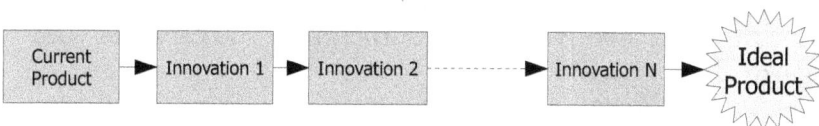

at each step needed to reach that ideal product from the current product.

Every Outcome has an ideal perfect criteria. As innovation occurs, each of the Outcomes moves closer to the Ideal State. The criterion needed for each successive innovation will be closer to that ideal until all the Outcomes achieve the theoretical maximum achievable state. This is why we don't specify the specific criterion for Outcomes when doing innovation. We are always trying to improve on the current level until we reach the ideal.

Each innovation improves one or more Outcomes enough to satisfy the emerging expectations. It is

> Do not get too far ahead of the market.

important to not try to offer products that are ahead of the market. Design products 2 steps ahead, develop products 1 step ahead, and deliver just-in-time. Products that are too far ahead will often require extra marketing expense to promote or won't have sufficiently advanced technology or infrastructure to affordably deliver the product.

To improve an Outcome an innovation must do one of the 3 things: maximize the State, minimize the State, or match a specific State. You will notice those are three of the five directions from the Alternatives Grid, Direct +, Indirect -, and Stable =.

You can improve an Outcome by increasing, decreasing, or equaling the desired result. For example, if the goal is to heat something, an innovation might be to decrease the time it takes to heat it. That would be minimizing the time.

Another way of improving an Outcome is to minimize, maximize, or match the range differences for the State. Instead of looking at a single State, a range of States might be desirable. When you select clothing you typically aren't maximizing or minimizing a look. You want clothing that can fit with a wide range of looks and work with other clothing you own. You want to maximize the range of your wardrobe.

Precision components must control size and position to fit together. However, it is not necessary to have the exact size and position as long as all the components are close to the same. The goal is to minimize the range of sizes and positions for all the components.

In the game of baseball the desired State is for the batter to hit the ball away from where players on the other team can catch it. This is a type of matching range. The criteria will use the words "not equals."

More on Outcomes

Outcomes are not an exact science. It takes significant practice to become proficient at writing Outcomes.

To quickly gain expertise in writing Outcomes attend a Predictive Innovation® workshop. The Predictive Innovation® website has a list of self-paced, instructor led online, and in-person training options to help you gain expertise.

http://www.PredictiveInnovation.com/

11.Components, Functions, and Outcomes

Products are made from Components. Components perform Functions to achieve the Outcomes the customer desires. Customers don't care about the Components or the Functions. All that customers want are the desired results for all of the Outcomes for their Scenario. This is why we focus on Outcomes.

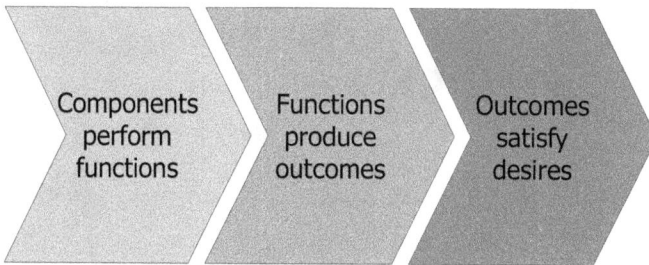

| Components perform functions | Functions produce outcomes | Outcomes satisfy desires |

Illustration 44: Product decomposition

Bicycles have many Components: wheels, frame, pedals, tires, seat, chain, gears, and handle bars. Each of these perform a different Function to achieve the overall Outcome of transportation.

A fork you eat with is generally made from a single material but has two Components, the prongs and the handle. The prongs collect and hold the food. The handle allows you to hold and move the fork.

Components are not necessarily physical. A book is made from paper, ink and glue but it is also made from words and punctuation. The physical ink on the paper form the words and punctuation but the words and punctuation themselves are not physical. The ink and paper alone don't convey meaning. The physical ink and paper arranged to form words and punctuation together perform the Function of communication.

The Function of a Component is determined by how it is used. When the product is originally designed, the Component has an intended Function. Modifications to the product or how it is used can change the Functions of a Component. Knives are often used to turn a screw even though they are not designed for that purpose.

Functions are focused on Actions. The combination of Functions form the process of satisfying a user's desires. More than one Component might be needed to perform a single Function and each Component could perform multiple Functions.

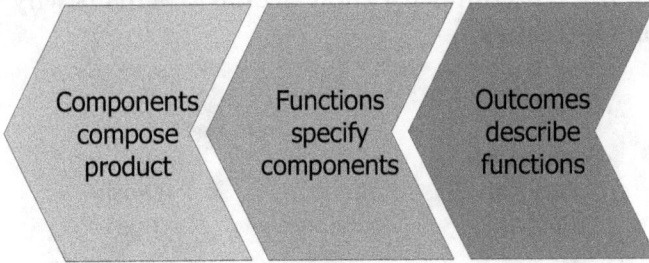

| Components compose product | Functions specify components | Outcomes describe functions |

Illustration 45: Product design up

When designing physical products, Components are most often represented with drawings that resemble the physical Objects. Component designs can range from rough drawings to highly detailed 3D computer aided designs (CAD). Since Functions are Actions and not physical Objects they are typically expressed as block diagrams that describe the process.

Recipes and driving directions are examples of Function diagrams.

Function Diagramming is very similar to Outcome Diagramming. You will use both for innovation work. Both Functions and Outcomes can be broken down into the same 7 Elements. The key difference is that Functions focus on Actions and Outcomes focus on States.

Predictive Innovation starts with Outcomes because that is the connection to customers and how we know the goal is achieved. Outcomes are what customers want. Functions are the technical process of achieving the Outcomes.

Consider the Outcome diagram of cookies and the Function Diagram of baking cookies. First thing you will notice is that the Function diagram is describing an Action, baking cookies.

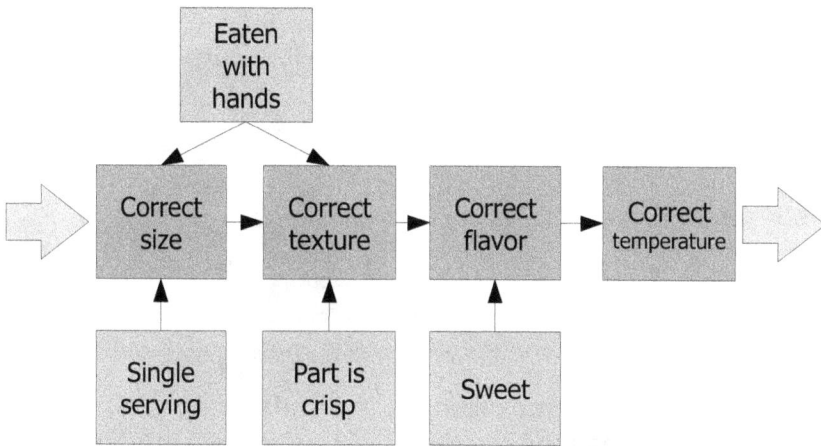

Illustration 46: Outcome Diagram for Cookies

The Outcome Diagram describes the characteristics of a cookie. A cookie must be the correct size, correct texture, correct flavor and correct temperature. The characteristics that distinguish a cookie from other food items are a single serving size, it can be eaten with hands, and part of it is crisp and, in the USA, the correct flavor is sweet. If you gave those criteria to someone who never saw a cookie they could recognize one and if they understood basic cooking they could possibly even make some variety of cookie.

A cookie is a cookie because it matches those criteria. It doesn't matter how those characteristics are achieved as long as the end product meets those requirements.

The Function Diagram is like a recipe. Function diagrams are focused on performing a task. Each of the Functions contributes to producing the end result we call a cookie.

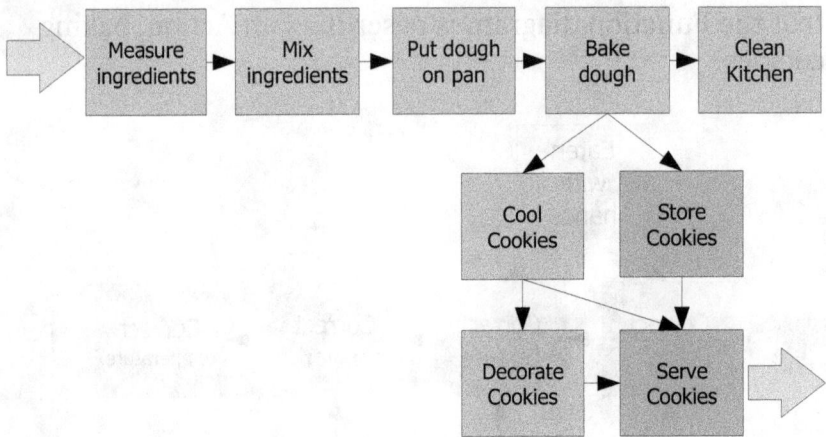

Illustration 47: Function Diagram for Baking Cookies

The Outcome diagram shows all the States that must exist to qualify as satisfying the desires of a cookie. Outcome Diagrams are customers' requirements. Function Diagrams are used to create the design. Designs show how the Components are assembled.

Engineers are trained to think in terms of Functions and Components and often will do the Functional analysis in their heads. That is good for a quick solution to a problem but it often misses valuable options.

It's always best to step back and start fresh with the customer's desires and the Outcomes that satisfy those desires. If you don't get the Desires and Outcomes your innovation options will be limited.

A customer might complain, "your product is too slow." If you jump to finding ways to make it faster you could miss why the customer wants it to be faster. Maybe the problem isn't your product being too slow but something else being too fast. Maybe when a step happens slowly it causes an undesired result that could be controlled another way, or the task isn't really needed at all. You can only get to those results by understanding the Outcomes that will satisfy the customer.

The general pattern of innovation is:

1. Outcome Diagram
2. Outcome Element Expansion
3. Alternatives Multiplication
4. Function Diagramming
5. Components Design

Product and Process Improvement

The main use of Function diagrams is product and process improvement. By looking at the steps and Components of a product or process you can isolate where to focus your attention for improvement. This is great for root cause of failure analysis.

There is a general rule of systems. Any single Component can be removed and still achieve the Function it performs. Approaches to eliminate a Component:

1. Have other Components perform the Function
2. Make the Function unneeded

If we look at the Outcomes Diagram you might find the Function is not needed. All of these approaches can be powerful ways to make innovations of products. Removing Components generally reduces cost and improves reliability by being less complex.

Complimentary Products

Function diagrams can be very useful for finding complimentary products. This can allow you to expand into another market while using the success of another product to grow the success of your product.

Steps to finding complimentary products:

1. Create a Function Diagram of your existing product

2. Compile a list of other products that perform one or more of the same Functions as your product.

3. Redesign or position your product to enhance, replace or use the Function of the other product so they become one system.

An example is a cell phone and car radio. Each receives a signal and plays sounds for the user to hear. Both the cell phone and car radio have Components that perform the same Function. Those Components could be shared to perform the Function for both. The radio can be the speakers of a speakerphone. Or the antenna of the radio can provide better reception for the phone. Or the color display on the phone could provide extra information about what is being played on the radio.

Exercise

Choose a product you regularly use. In a single sentence describe one Scenario you use the product.

Make three lists.

1. List what desires the product satisfies. Express the desires objectively if you can.

2. List the steps or Functions performed to satisfy the desire.

3. To the best of your ability, list the Components in the product.

Once you have the three lists try to map Components to Functions and Functions to Outcomes or desires.

- Are there any Components that don't directly map to your desires?

- Are there any Components or Functions that detract from satisfying your desires?

Practice this exercise with every product and service you encounter.

12.Primary Elements

If you break something down to it's smallest pieces those pieces are the primary elements.

Every book, paragraph, sentence, and word in English can be broken down into 26 letters plus a few punctuation marks. These are the primary elements of the written English language.

Arithmetic can be broken down to addition or subtraction. Multiplication is repeated addition. Division is repeated subtraction. [7]

Colors can be broken down to three primary colors, blue, red, and yellow. All other colors are made from those three.

Primary Colors

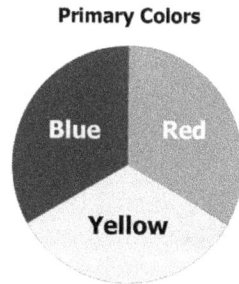

Methods for achieving goals can also be broken down into primary elements.

Using the primary components you can find all the possible ways of achieving the goal. Breaking a system down into primary elements makes it easy to understand. By combining all the elements you can find large amounts of options. More importantly, these options are organized so you can easily work with and understand all of them.

Take the example of shoes. Let say there are two choices of color: black, white. And there are three styles: flats, high heel, and sandal. When we put the choices into a matrix we find all the combinations.

---

7 All information processing can be reduced to repeated comparisons using, either NAND or NOR operations. This is called Turing Complete.

	Black	White
Flats	1	2
Heels	3	4
Sandal	5	6

2 colors x 3 styles = 6 options

If we add another color the number of options doesn't increase by one but by the number of choices for the other variable.

	Black	Red	White
Flats	1	2	3
Heels	4	5	6
Sandal	7	8	9

3 colors x 3 styles = 9 options

If we add another dimension the number of options expands even more quickly. Lets add material with two options, leather and cloth.

Shoes	Leather			Cloth		
	Black	Red	White	Black	Red	White
Flats	1	2	3	10	11	12
Heels	4	5	6	13	14	15
Sandal	7	8	9	16	17	18

3 colors x 3 styles x 2 materials = 18

In a few easy steps we described 18 shoe combinations. We chose 3 dimensions: Color, Style, and Material.

Now think of all the options available for each dimension. More colors, more materials, more styles?

How many dimensions can you add? Size, designer, store?

Adding dimensions is where you get the big increases in options.

Bicycle Examples

How many dimensions are there on a bicycle? If we only look at the physical components of a bicycle we can come up with a good sized list. Without getting too detailed I can come up with 9 components of a bicycle.

· wheels	· seat	· brakes
· tires	· frame	· pedals
· handle bars	· gears	· forks

Now that we have the components list, or variables, how many choices can we think of for each one of those variables? Add your own to the list.

Variable	Choice	
Wheels	• Solid	•
	• Spokes	•
	• Plastic	•
	• Steel	•
	• Magnesium	•
	• Fixed	•
	• Removable	•
Tires	• Thin	•
	• Thick	•
	• Smooth tread	•
	• Knobby tread	•
	• Solid	•
Handle bars	• Upright	•
	• Curved under	•
	• Padded	•
Seat	• Narrow	•
	• Wide	•
	• Split	•
Frame	• Boys	•
	• Girls	•
	• Steel	•
	• Aluminum	•
	• Carbon fiber	•
Gears	• Single speed	•
	• Multiple speed	•
	• Steel	•
	• Magnesium	•

Brakes	• Coaster	•
	• Caliper	•
	• Disc	•
Forks	• Straight	•
	• Curved	•
	• Solid	•
	• Shock absorber	•
Pedals	• Open	•
	• Toe grip	•

The list I provided had 39 options. How many things did you add to the list?

If you look at the list you will notice that a few choices showed up more than once, such as Steel, Aluminum, and Magnesium. Each of those are a material. We could add the variable "material" to our matrix and apply that to all the choices.

How many different types of materials can you think of?

> • Metal   • Wood   • Glass
> • Plastic   • Fabric   • Stone

That list of materials is not specific; it is a list of categories of materials. In effect we zoomed in to get more detail. You can zoom in or zoom out to get the level of detail that is helpful for what you are doing at the moment. Breaking things down into dimensions provides structure to guide your thinking and keeps the results organized.

If we had started with listing very specific materials like white oak, 440C steel, or wool tweed, it would be very easy to overlook options. We would also spend a lot of time listing options that might not be helpful. Focusing at the correct level provides structure that makes creativity easier.

Chunking

Neuro-Linguistic
Programming (NLP)
calls this process of
choosing the right level
of detail chunking. You
break things down or
group them together
into the appropriate
sized chunk. Breaking
things into smaller
chunks is called
chunking down.
Stepping back and

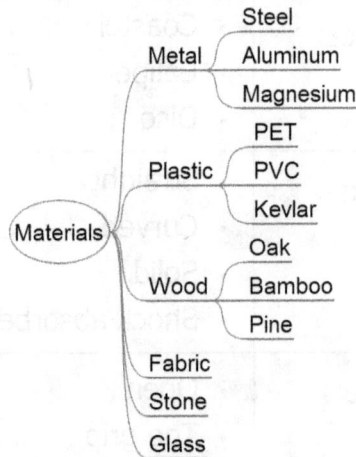

Illustration 48: Material Chunking Levels

looking at bigger chunks is called chunking up. Learning
how to chunk is very useful for innovating.

The key to chunking is choosing a dimension then move up
or down by levels. Illustration 48 shows three different
levels. Wood, plastic, and metal are at one level and steel,
aluminum, and magnesium are at a lower level.

Unstructured brainstorming quickly slows down because
you have to spend a lot of time thinking about what you
already have. Going about it in a systematic way we can
easily come up with hundreds of materials.

If we add more categories and chunk down we can quickly
and easily list thousands of options. Looking back at the
bicycle here are just a few more categories for the physical
aspects of the parts.

- Size
- Shape
- Weight
- Color
- Density
- Purity

Notice that each of those categories could apply to the
physical aspect of many different items.

For some things it is possible to choose the correct
dimension and chunk size so that you can describe every
option. For instance you can describe every color using
three dimensions: hue, saturation, and luminance. You

probably learned as a child that all the colors are combinations of red, yellow and blue. That is not technically correct. Mixing standard shades of red, yellow, and blue will provide every hue but it does not provide every shade. It doesn't make lighter

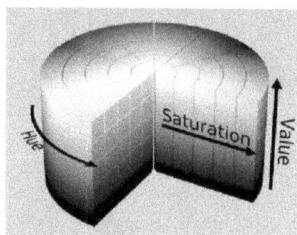

Illustration 49: HSV Color Cylinder

muted tones like pink or the vivid neon shades. The red, yellow, blue model is missing the ranges. If you mix the full range of each of the primary colors then you can get every color. This can be represented by three numbers ranging from 0 to 100%. Zero for all three is black, 100% for all three is white. The various combinations result in every other color possible.

When you have properly defined the correct dimensions you can describe all the possible combinations for that item. You know all the extremes in every direction, what is and what is not your item. You understand the full range between the extremes; that is all the combinations.

In the case of colors it would be impossible to make a list of each individual color. Using the three dimensions of hue, saturation and luminance you can easily describe all the colors. This is the same way Predictive Innovation works.

13. Elements

In the bicycle example on page 91, we broke down the bicycle into components, then each component into categories of materials, shapes, sizes, etc. That helped us increase our choices but it didn't really focus our thoughts very well. We just ended up with a long list of options. We need to define the correct dimensions so that we cover the full range.

How can we use the technique of primary elements for innovation?

You've seen the 15 Alternatives, which are arranged into Scale and Direction. And you've seen how to convert subjective desires into objective Outcomes. Applying the 15 Alternatives directly to Outcomes is not enough structure. If we chunk down Outcomes into the 7 Elements, we have exactly what we need to describe every innovation for a specific Scenario.

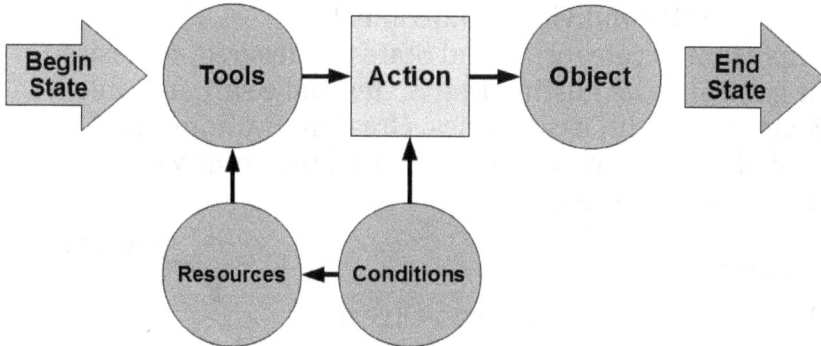

Illustration 50: 7 Elements of an Outcome

Object

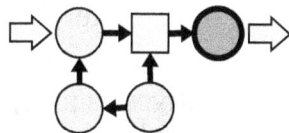

Object is the property or event of the Outcome. The Object is what makes the Outcome objective. Objects are nouns. Innovation can be achieved by using non-obvious Objects. For instance if the problem is heat you might focus on the shape since Objects with more surface area dissipate heat better than more regular shaped Objects. Similarly by changing the color an Object might absorb less heat.

Predictive Innovation website resources section has an extensive list of scientific properties and the units of measurement.

Begin State

The Begin State is the State or quality that exists before you start. This is what you are either trying to change or keep. States are adjectives describing the Object. States can be described with a number and unit, or a descriptive word such as blue, harder, taller, or solid. State can also be an event recognized as occurring or not occurring.

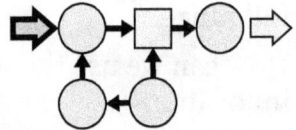

End State

The End State is the result of the Action for the individual Outcome. It's important to categorize End States as: desired, undesired, or neutral. When listing End States make sure to think of States for all three categories. Great innovations are available from preventing undesired results as well as making desired results.

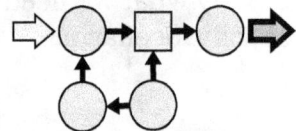

Action

Actions cause the State of an Object. The Action is the "how" you achieve the goal. The Action causes the State to change or stay the same. Actions are verbs.

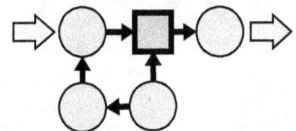

Examples of Actions are: cut, join, separate, divide, mix, sort, order, filter, blend, melt, freeze, thaw, or heat.

When listing Actions think of the first 3 Direction Alternatives as plus, minus, and equals. Cutting might be considered a plus since it makes more pieces, gluing together makes less pieces, and turning the Object around leaves the number of pieces the same.

In addition to common verbs there are hundreds of scientific effects that can be used to perform Actions.

Visit the resources section of Predictive Innovation website to see an extensive list of verbs and scientific effects to help you think of Actions.

Tools

Tool is directly used to help perform the Action. A Tool can be a physical item or a process. Algebra and language are Tools. A Tool interacts with the Object. If the Action is cut, the Tool might be a: saw, knife, torch, scissors, or laser. Each of those Tools can be used to perform the Action of cutting.

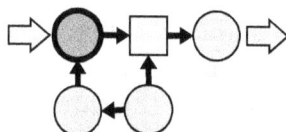

Conditions

Conditions are any State or quality that effects achieving the Outcome.
Conditions affect but are not directly related to the Outcome. The age of the tea leaves or the pH of the water could affect the result of brewing but isn't directly related to brewing. Wet pavement or riding on sand affects a bicycles ability to move and stop.

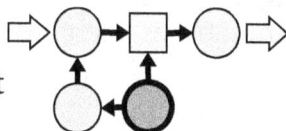

Resources

A Resource is anything available in the environment of the Scenario that can be used to help achieve the result. Resources are not just materials. Information, people, or other components are all possible Resources. When brewing tea, being able to measure the age of tea leaves is a Resource. A chart of times to brew different blends at different temperatures is another Resource. A spoon is a Resource that can be used to stir the tea and better brew the tea. Gravity is another very useful Resource. Resources are potential Tools. It's up to you to find uses for available Resources.

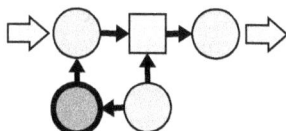

Element Expansion

Element expansion is the process of breaking down the Outcomes into the 7 Elements. This is where you begin to find all the innovations. Each Outcome has at least one of each of the 7 Elements.

You need to identify the Outcome you will change to solve the problem or find innovations. For problems there is usually a dilemma. A dilemma is when improving one desired Outcome results in worsening another desired Outcome. You can select either Outcome of a dilemma to focus your work. For innovation, focus on one Outcome at a time.

If you are having trouble drawing an Outcome diagram, it is sometimes useful to start by listing Elements.

When you are first learning to draw Outcome diagrams or when facilitating other people, it can be easier to list Objects, States, and Action then reorganize these into concise Outcomes. Many people are accustomed to brainstorming and will want to use a more free form process to get started.

You can keep the task relatively focused by directing efforts towards the scenario and listing meaningful Objects, States, Actions, and Conditions. This will often help you clarify your thoughts. This is also a good way to capture ideas for solutions for later consideration.

Until you've properly defined the Outcomes you can't evaluate any idea. This is why people put so much emphasis on not judging ideas during a brainstorming session and saying, "there is no such thing as a bad idea." There clearly are bad ideas and it is very important to judge ideas before investing any time or money. Until you have objective criteria you would only be guessing if you judged the ideas. If you are listing Elements to help you define Outcomes just record all free form ideas because there is no point in overlooking the obvious ideas.

Once you have drawn an Outcome diagram, select the Outcome you want

Focus on one Outcome at a time

to change then begin by listing Objects for that Outcome. Next list the begin and End States for the Object making sure to note desired, undesired, and neutral States.

Now choose one Object and the States that apply. Look at each Begin State and list Actions that will cause the End States. For problem solving you will often find solutions at this point. For innovation make a note of Actions that seem particularly promising but continue with the process so you won't miss potentially better ideas or complimentary approaches that will help build a strategy for entire product families.

Once you have Actions listed for the States you can list Tools that help perform those Actions.

Finally list Conditions and Resources related to the Action. Review Tools and Actions as you add Conditions and Resources.

Summary of Element Expansion

1. Select an Outcome to improve.
2. Choose an Object.
3. List begin and End States for the Object, noting desired, undesired, a neutral States.
4. List Actions to cause each Begin State to become an End State.
5. List Tools for each Action.
6. List Conditions affecting the performance of the Action.
7. List Resources that could be used to perform the Action.

Element Example: Cookies

There are 4 main Outcomes and 4 sub-Outcomes in Illustration 51: Outcome Diagram for Cookies. The first step for innovation is to select an Outcome to improve. Lets choose Correct Size. This Outcome has two sub-Outcomes, eaten with hands and single serving. The sub-Outcomes provide extra restrictions that we must work within.

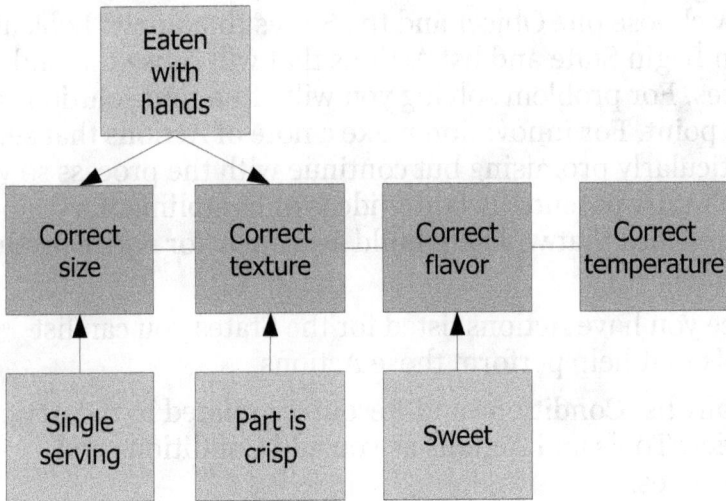

Illustration 51: Outcome Diagram for Cookies

Cookies can be given as gifts, looked at, sold for a profit, or eaten. We have to consider the scenario of how we are using cookies to properly think of Outcomes. If we think about cookies as food we can draw a very simple diagram with only 4 Outcomes. All of the Outcomes of a cookie must come together for it to be eaten and enjoyed thus satisfying the hunger of the person who eats it.

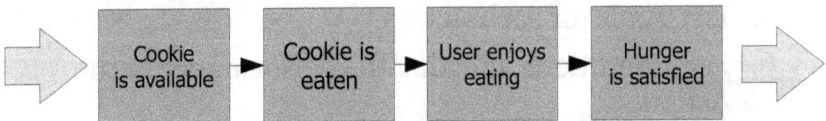

Illustration 52: Outcome Diagram for Eating Cookies

While we are expanding the Outcomes of cookies consider that each Outcome fits into the scenario of eating cookies. The correct size, correct texture, correct flavor, and correct temperature combine to make the cookie available, and enjoyably eaten.

Choose Object

Once you have selected the Outcomes, the next step is to choose an Object. What are the Objects of the Correct Size Outcome?

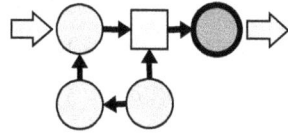

- width of cookie
- height of cookie
- length of cookie
- weight of cookie
- shape of the cookie

These are the obvious Objects but there is also:

- hands

- mouth

- packaging

Coming up with the lists of Elements is where you can use your imagination. Chunking [8] can be a very useful technique for listing Elements.

Remember to consider the less obvious Elements. Cookies made for adults could be different sizes than cookies made for children. Also cookies might not be made for people at all so there are many other ways to look at this Outcome.

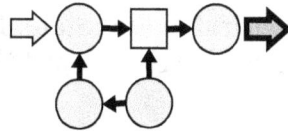

Define Desired End States

The shape of the cookie is affected by each individual size. We need to consider all of the sizes together because combined sizes makes the shape. Changing one of the sizes without considering the other sizes could adversely alter the shape.

A cookie that is too wide won't fit into your mouth because it hits the sides of your mouth. A flat round or flat square

---

8 Chunking page 94

cookie could be too wide to eat. It could also be too wide to hold in your hands. If the cookie was soft and too wide it might droop over the sides of your hand. That problem often happens with slices of pizza.

A cookie with a height that is too much won't fit in your mouth because you can't open your mouth enough.

A cookie that is too long won't fit in your mouth when you close it, plus it could sag around your hands like a slice of pizza.

It is unlikely that a cookie would be too heavy to eat but the weight might effect serving sizes and a cookie which is too light might be considered undesirable.

States can be desirable, undesirable, or neutral. There are four ways a State can be desirable, undesirable, or neutral:

- too much
- too little
- matching
- not matching

The Begin States and End States for cookies sizes are similar. The goal is for any undesirable Begin State to be a desirable End State. It is not important to list all the possible States, just the relevant States.

Undesirable	Neutral	Desirable
• Cookie width is too much • Cookie width is too small • Cookie height is too large • Cookie height is too small • Cookie length is too large • Cookie length is too small	• Modifiable • liquid or gel • Separate ingredients	• Correct size for hands • Correct size for mouth • Long and narrow • Small round disc • Small flat square • Small ball • Small cube

Correct width, correct height, and correct length are the desired States. The correct width, height and length will vary depending on each other. A cookie can have a larger height if the width is not large. The overall combination of shape and size result in the cookie being the desired correct size or an undesired or neutral size. The correct size is one that allows the cookie to be picked up with your hands, put in your mouth and eaten.

If the cookie is the wrong size for hands or mouth but could be easily modified that is a neutral State. An example is a cookie that can be easily broken in to pieces that are the correct size.

List Actions

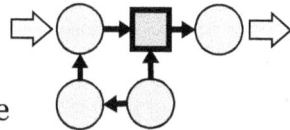

What are the Actions to make the cookie the correct size? The correct size for the mouth is different than the correct size for the hand. An obvious Action for making a cookie the correct size for the mouth is biting it. The cookie still needs to be the correct size for biting and must be the correct size for the hands. The various shapes of a cookie can result from different Actions.

Chocolate chip cookies are made into flat discs by measuring an amount of dough and baking it. The heat causes the dough to spread and form the shape. Sugar cookies are made into fancy shapes like hearts and stars by using a mold with the dough. Soft cookies could also be cut into shapes after they are baked. Many manufactured cookies are molded to have thin spots making them easier to break into smaller pieces. Cylindrical cookies can be molded, rolled, or folded before baking or in the middle of the process.

Look at each Begin State and each desired or neutral End State then list all the Actions that can result in a desired or neutral End State.

· Measure	· Fold	· Squeeze
· Mold	· Break	· Bite
· Cut	· Roll	· Soak

Measuring, molding, or cutting the dough can make the correct size and shape. Breaking, biting, and cutting can make a baked cookie the correct size and shape. Notice that we just introduced another State, baked and dough before baked.

So, we find that there are other States such as before the cookie is baked and after. Those States aren't part of the overall Outcome of Cookie, those are intermediary States related to the Action of making cookies.

Remember that Outcome Diagrams focus on States. Function Diagrams focus on Actions. Eventually you will want to create Function Diagrams for each Action. If you discover new information while listing Actions record it for later use.

Resist jumping into designing a solution at this stage. You will find many more options which might be more effective and less costly. Since the Element Expansion is quick and easy don't skip it. Complete the full process before deciding which solution you will use. A little thought can save a lot of work.

Look at the Action soak. Dipping a cookie in milk or tea is a popular way to eat cookies. A soft cookie is easier to eat. The size and shape of the cookie affects the ability to soak it. Long cylindrical cookies are much easier to soak than spherical balls. The long cylindrical cookie is too long to put completely in your mouth but it is perfect for dipping which then makes it easier to bite and eat. Soaking also points out other Objects such as the cup and liquid you are soaking the cookie in.

As we are listing Actions we discovered more Objects and States and related Outcomes. We also found the connection to Function Diagrams for baking cookies. That is exactly what we want to do. Don't worry about finding all the Elements at each stage. Write down all the information you gather and continue with the process. This may involve going back to previous steps and adding or changing what you had before. As you better understand the scenario you will be better able to describe it and thus all the innovations. The systematic approach will help you reveal all the options.

List Tools

Tools are physical and non-physical items that are directly used in performing Actions. These are usually quite easy to list. For example, a cookie cutter helps you cut or mold a cookie into the correct shape and size.

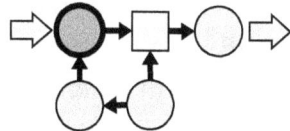

Action	Tool
Measure	Cup, spoon, scale
Mold	Mold, pan, nozzle
Cut	Knife, saw, burner, scissors, die
Fold	Edge
Break	Edge, scored line
Roll	Board, sheet
Squeeze	Press, mold, rolling pin
Bite	Teeth, jaw,
Soak	Cup, spoon

List Conditions

Conditions are any State that may affect the ability to produce the desired State or changes which State is desired.

The ingredients of a cookie affect that ability to make it the correct size and shape. Temperature could also affect the size and shape. If the cookie is frozen it might make it more or less difficult to bite or break into pieces that fit in your mouth.

Where and when are very common Conditions. Eating cookies for a snack at work is different from being at home which is different from being at a party. Who is eating the cookie changes what size is correct. A child's hands and mouth are different from an adult.

- Temperature
- Ingredients
- Moisture
- Size of mouth
- Size of hands
- Ingredients
- Where eaten
- When eaten
- Who you are eating with

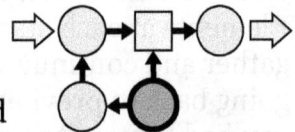

List Resources

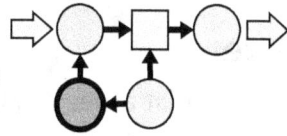

A Resource is anything available in the environment of the scenario that can help achieve the Outcome. The temperature could be useful for cutting or breaking a cookie. Knowing the temperature could be helpful for preparing and serving cookies. Knowing the moisture levels could also be helpful.

- Serving plate
- Wrapper, container
- Dishes
- Cup
- Temperature of the cookie
- Temperature of hands, mouth, room

Next Step

Just listing Elements does not find all the options. The first pass gives you something to work with. Multiplying Alternatives for each of the Elements shows you the ideas you did not find.

Exercise

1. List at least 3 Objects that are important to listening to music.

2. List States for the volume Object of listening to music.

3. What Actions can be used to affect the volume of music?

4. What Conditions affect the volume of music?

5. What Tools can be used to affect the volume of music?

6. What are some Resources related to listening to music on an MP3 player?

14.Multiplying Alternatives

When you have Elements for all the Outcomes you want to work on, it's time to multiply Alternatives. For problem solving projects describe Alternatives for Elements until you find a suitable solution. For innovation projects describe at least one of each of the 15 Alternatives for each element. This will generate 105 ideas for each Outcome. Since most scenarios have approximately 7 Outcomes you will have approximately 735 focused ideas organized into categories by Outcomes, Elements, and Alternatives. This will help you develop strategies.

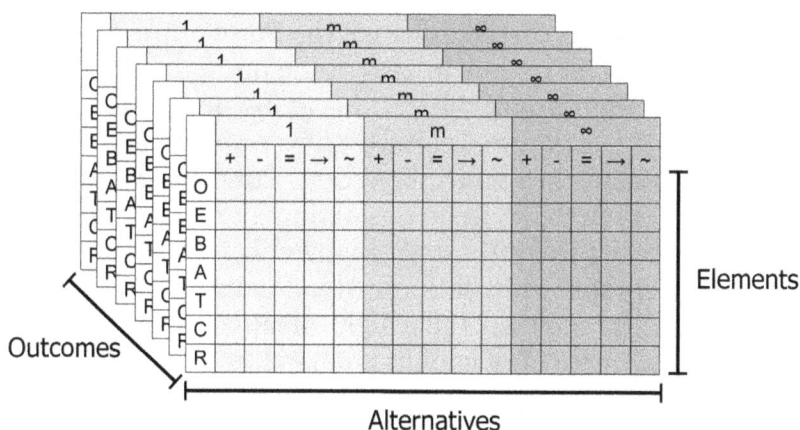

Illustration 53: 735 Focused Ideas

Each of the 105 innovation combinations for an Outcome are a type. There can be many different specific innovations for each type. The type is a description of an approach to achieving the Outcome. There can be many specific ways that fit the description.

Many of the Alternatives will have existing products or services. If you find an Alternative that has not been used it is a potential disruptive breakthrough innovation. The description of the other breakthroughs exist with Alternatives that were used in the past but not currently used. Newer technology can make those Alternative approaches achieve better results than current approaches.

Start Multiplying Alternatives by selecting from the list of Actions then describe an example for each of the 15 Alternatives. To help you get started find the box that an existing product fits such as Single Direct, then describe Multiple Direct and Continuous Direct for that product.

As you describe Alternatives you may find boxes that you can't think of examples to match the descriptions. Do not expect to be able to find examples for each box; in fact you want to find boxes that don't have examples. The empty boxes are the future innovations. Describe what should be in those boxes. The description will guide your innovations.

Direct Alternatives are usually the most obvious approach. Those Alternatives directly change the State of the Object. One example of a Single Direct is doing an Action to the Object once. Similarly if the Action can be performed in a single step, it is a Single. Multiple steps or being able to do it more than once is a multiple Action. Continuous is any, all, or none. Being able to do the Action an unlimited number of times is continuous. Being able to perform the Action in a smooth application instead of many steps is continuous. For cookies, that might mean an oven with a conveyor belt instead of cooking in batches.

	Direct +	Indirect -	Keep Stable =	Make Stable →	Return to Stable ~
Single					
Multiple					
Continuous					

Example: Cookie Size

Size and shape are related Objects. Many different Actions and Tools can be used to change the size or shape of a cookie.

Direct

	+	-	=	→	~
1					
m					
∞					

Single

Bite once, bite one direction

Single cut, perform cut once

Mold one shape or size, mold used one (disposable)

Measure one cookie at a time, measure a single size, measure in one step, measure one material

Multiple

Bite multiple times, bite more than one direction

Multiple cuts, perform cut multiple times

Mold multiple shapes or sizes, mold used multiple times

Measure multiple cookies at a time, measure multiple sizes, measure in multiple steps, measure multiple materials

Continuous

Never bite, bite any direction, bite all directions

Cuts all (powder, liquid), perform cut unlimited times

Mold any shape or size, mold used multiple times

Measure any number of cookies at a time, measure all the cookies from a batch at a time, continuously measure (flow measurement, measure throughout process), measure any size, measure any material, measure all materials

Indirect

	+	-	=	→	~
1					
m					
∞					

Single

Not bite (completely fits in mouth, one cookie, one eater or type of eater), Bite different item, Cookie used to bite

Not cut (only weaken), Puncture, Cookie cuts something.

Create shape without molding, Dough applied to outside of something to create shape. Mouth is mold, forms to hand (squeeze), Cookie molds something else

Don't measure, measure effect instead of cookie (displacement of liquid or gas)

Multiple

Not bite multiple cookies (very small put many in mouth at once)

Many perforations, many thin spots to ease breaking

Create many shapes without a mold. Apply dough to outside of multiple Objects to create shape. Applied to outside in multiple ways.

Measure multiple other things, use cookie to do measurement

Continuous

Never bite, cookie is soft enough to eat without biting regardless of size.

Cut: Cookie cuts anything

Mold: Cookie dough sticks to outside of any shape

Measure: Never measure because you know it is correct, statistical process control (SPC)

Keep Stable

	+	-	=	→	~
1					
m					
∞					

Single

Keep one cookie the correct size, packaging prevents breakage

Keep rest of cookie together when biting off a piece, doesn't crumble or crack.

Keep the cuts the correct size

Mold, stays correct size and shape

Measure, measure doesn't change

Multiple

Keep many cookies the correct size, packaging prevents breakage for many cookies, or many Conditions.

Keep cookies separate, many cookies.

Keep many cuts the correct size. Keep cookie the correct size or shape after multiple cuts.

Mold stays the correct size and shape many times.

Measure stays the same many times. Many measurements don't change.

Continuous

All the cookies are the correct size or shape.

All the cookies are kept separated.

Every cut is correct. Cuts are always correct.

Mold lasts forever. Mold works for any type of cookie.

Measurement continuous adjusted to stay correct.

Make Stable

	+	-	=	→	~
1					
m					
∞					

Single

Cookies become correct size. Shrink as they cool.

Cookie becomes shape of the package.

As the cookie cooks it becomes the correct shape.

Multiple

Cookies can become many sizes. Able to select the size to which the cookie shrinks when it cools.

Cookies form to packages with many different shapes.

Many different shaped molds that cookies become the shape of as they cook.

Several different shaped nozzles on a tube of pre-made cookie dough.

Continuous

Always becomes correct size.

All the cookies become the correct size or shape.

Cookies can become any shape. 3D printer makes nozzles of any shape for the tube of pre-made cookie dough.

Return to Stable

	+	-	=	→	∼
1					
m					
∞					

Single
Mold can be repaired one time.

Single size or shape can change and return to correct size or shape.

Multiple
Mold can be repaired many times.

Cookie can change size many times and return to correct size.

Continuous
Mold can always be repaired.

Cookie can be shaped any number of times.

Exercise

Register online for free answer sheets to all exercises

1. List ways to use each of the Scales (Single, Multiple, Continuous) to make a product:

    - cheaper
    - higher priced
    - more reliable
    - easier to build

2. List Indirect opposite approaches to making something fit.

3. Choose and product or service then list Indirect Opposite ways of achieving the same goal.

4. List Indirect Opposite goal.

5. List examples of: hold, protect, store

6. Which Directions focus on periods of time?

7. List examples of Return to Stable for:

    - Quantitative
    - Qualitative
    - Physical
    - Conceptual

15.Universal User Process

There is a universal process that applies to using any product. These are the general steps done to use any product or service. The universal process starts with deciding to use the product and ends when you have completed what you used the product to achieve and you have put the product away or disposed of it. If you are looking for innovations this is a simple way to find things about your product that can be improved.

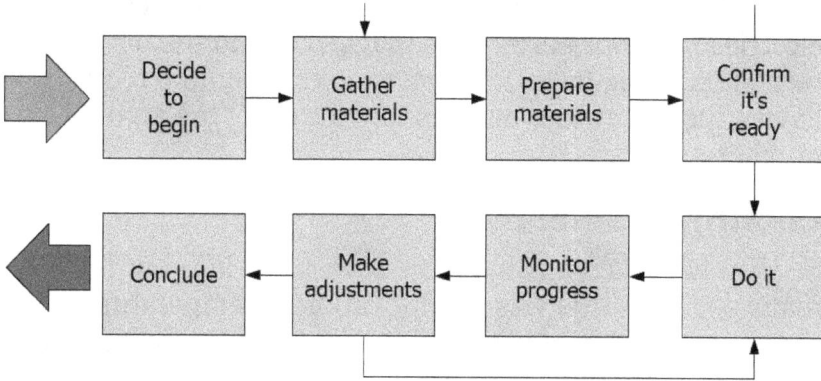

Illustration 54: Universal User Process Diagram

Notice that the Universal User Process Diagram is not an Outcome diagram; it is a process or Function diagram. It shows the actions taken. An Outcome diagram shows the States that must be achieved. Without a specific goal, most people find it easier to imagine using a product than the results. For each step in the process there are Outcomes for measuring how well it is done.

Decide to Begin

Something happens that causes you to use a product. Helping a user know when to use a product and that the product is the way to achieve their desire is an important aspect with many potential innovations.

Gather Materials

Once you've decided to begin the task you need to gather all materials for doing the task, including non-physical items such as lists of information or measures.

Prepare Materials

Often the materials related to using a product are not ready when you get them. You might need to take them out of a package, put them in some order or position, clean, or otherwise get them ready to start using the product. An electric appliance needs to be plugged in and the power turned on to the outlet. Buying something online requires having money in your account and knowing the account number or password.

Confirm It's Ready

Confirming it is ready to use may seem obvious but for many products that was an innovation. A temperature gauge on the oven tells you it is ready to begin cooking. A power light on a device shows you it has power and is turned on.

Do It

The do it step is different for each product. This step is described by a complete Function and Outcome diagram for the specific product.

Monitor Progress

You need to know if the product is working, if you need to change how you are using it, or if it is done. Many products on the market could be improved in the monitor progress step.

Make Adjustments

Based on the information from the monitor progress step you might make adjustments. At some point you make the final adjustment of ending using the product because you have completed what you were doing.

Conclude

When you are done you need to put away the product, materials and clean up any mess. You might also need to buy more to be ready for next time. And concluding using one product might start the process over again with deciding to use a different product.

16.Problem Solving

Problem solving is a type of innovation. I prefer to use the term "solution finding" instead of problem solving. All the solutions can be described using Predictive Innovation. If all you need is one practical solution then you don't need to use the entire method.

The key difference between solution finding and more general innovation work is the difference of Scale. For innovation you want many or all the solutions. For solution finding you only need one solution to be satisfied.

The same techniques used to find solutions are used to uncover innovations but your efforts are more focused and the process doesn't take as long. All you need is a single change to solve the problem.

Solving the Unsolvable

Most unsolvable problems have the form that there are two desired results and it seems that the only way to improve one is to make the other worse. It's a dilemma. Unsolvable dilemmas are the result of an incorrect assumptions. With this simple understanding the obvious solution is to correct the inaccurate assumption and then reapply problem solving techniques.

The five steps to solving dilemmas are:

1. Describe dilemma
2. Find assumptions
3. Identify latent generalizations in the assumptions
4. Invert each word
5. Reveal opportunities matching the new understanding

Dilemma

All seemingly unsolvable problems are
the result of some dilemma. You want
to improve both X and Y but improving
one makes the other worse. Unless the
dilemma violates a fundamental law of physics, it is the
result of a mistaken assumption or an excessive
generalization.

Assumptions

Assumptions are beliefs that might not be true. So, you
need to confirm that what you believe is actually true.

There are three types of assumptions:

• Assumptions of Result

• Assumptions of Approach

• Emotional Assumptions

If any of these assumptions are incorrect it can result in a
dilemma. Exposing an incorrect assumption is often all that
is needed to reveal solutions.

Assumptions of Result are criteria we assume are needed to
achieve the goal. A dilemma can occur when an
unnecessary criteria is assumed. Unnecessary criteria could
be totally unneeded or could be overly restrictive criteria.
An example is requiring a tool be a specific color even
though it will end up dirty and the color hidden.

Another Assumption of Result is an unstated assumption.
These often happen when the real purpose is not properly
defined. If your goal is to reduce the time spent traveling to
work you might Assume the Result is finding a home closer
to your job. You might be equally happy if you worked 4

days per week instead of five. It's important to define the criteria properly.

Assumptions of Approach are the result of not considering Alternative ways of achieving the result. A common assumption of approach is trying to do something in a single step or with a single piece when it is possible to break it up into multiple steps or pieces.

The classic Assumption of Approach is the myth of Alexander and the Gordian knot. In the myth, whoever loosed the supposed impossible to untie Gordian knot would become ruler of the world. Everyone who attempted to untie the knot was unable. Alexander also tried and in frustration took out his sword and cut the

Illustration 55: Alexander cutting the Gordian Knot

knot in half. The criteria was to loosen the knot, there wasn't any rule against cutting it. He overcame the Assumption of Approach, solved the problem, and went on to rule the known world.

Unstated assumptions frequently contribute to Assumptions of Approach. Make sure to ask your self "Why am I doing this?" and "What will this allow me to do?" If you say, "I must" or "I should" state the reason for that "must" and "should", this will help you avoid unstated assumptions.

Emotional Assumptions are strong emotional reactions that are not relevant to achieving the actual goal. That causes people to overlook valid Alternatives or make other assumptions that interfere with achieving the stated result. Emotional Assumptions often appear as unstated assumptions. A person will object to solutions but not provide a valid reason.

Often the Emotional Assumptions can be resolved by correcting Assumptions of Result or Approach.

Deeply engrained Emotional Assumptions can be resolved using techniques like NLP, Neuro-Linguistic Programming. NLP is itself an Outcome Driven approach for altering emotional responses. NLP often requires only a single session to resolve even the most extreme cases such as phobias and Post-Traumatic-Stress Disorder (PTSD). Recognizing and having techniques for dealing with Emotional Assumptions can be very helpful when facilitating innovation.

Following the Predictive Innovation model can help you avoid all of the assumptions by giving you an unemotional orderly structure to follow.

Generalizations

A generalization is a belief that is true for some Conditions but not for all the Conditions. Generalizations can cause you to miss seeing possible solutions. The Scales of the Alternatives grid is very useful for spotting generalizations.

Inversion

Since we naturally tend to focus on the Direct solutions, a quick way to test assumptions is to find Indirect Alternatives. Inversion is a quick shortcut for finding Indirect Alternatives. To use inversion, state your assumption then reverse or invert each part.

Example:

> I need a new suit to get a job; but,
> I need a job to afford a new suit.

This dilemma has two parts or clauses that contradict each other. Both clauses have an Assumed Result and an Assumed Approach.

Start by inverting each word of the first clause.

> I **don't** <u>**need**</u> a new suit to get a job.

The assumption is that a suit is required. A suit might make it easier to get a job but is it really needed to get a job? That is also a generalization. Are there ways of getting jobs that don't need a suit? There is a generalization that all jobs require a suit. Are there jobs that don't need a new suit?

> I **don't** need a <u>**new**</u> suit to get a job.

The assumption is the suit must be new. Does the suit need to be new or do you just need a suit? Could you wear a used suit to get the job? There is a generalization that the entire suit be new. Could your suit be modified to make it new? Perhaps you can alter the collar width to make it look new.

> I **don't** need a new <u>**suit**</u> to get a job.

The assumption is that a suit is the only way to dress to get a job. Would a nice shirt and tie work? There is a generalization that you need a whole suit. Do you need the whole suit or just a new jacket or new pants or skirt?

> I **don't** need a new suit to <u>**get**</u> a job.

There is an assumption and generalization about the order of events. Do you only need the suit to get the job and not to do the work? Can you get the job before getting the suit? After you get the job do you still need the suit?

> I **don't** need a new suit to get <u>**a job**</u>.

The assumption is your end goal is the job. Do you need a job or do you need money? Do you need money or do you need something money can buy? The generalization is the goal can't be broken up into steps. Could you get one job that doesn't need the suit so you can get the suit to get the job that does require the suit?

> <u>**I**</u> **don't** need a new suit to get a job.

There is an assumption and generalization that you own the suit. Does the suit have to be yours? Could you borrow a suit? Could you rent the suit? Could you buy the suit then return it after the interview? Could you share the cost of a suit with a friend? The generalization is all the Resources available belong to you. Could you borrow the money to buy the suit? Could someone else get the job? Perhaps you could get a roommate to pay the bills.

We focused on the first clause but the inversions generated answers covered much of the other clause as well. If you get good answers by inverting only one clause you can stop. If you want more it's quick and easy to invert both clauses to find the solution you want.

The inversion shortcut found Alternatives for the Object and the Action and hinted at some Tools. Since we were just trying to find one solution we didn't go through all the steps of listing all the Outcomes, expanding into Elements and finding Alternatives.

This problem had several incorrect assumptions but it also had an Unstated Assumption. Why did the person need a job? Was there something they wanted to buy? Did they need a job to impress someone? Would having a job help them meet people? Did they need a job to fill out a credit application for renting an apartment? The Unstated Assumption could totally change the criteria and approaches.

Making sure you are solving the correct problem is another way to solve seemingly unsolvable problems. If you are trying to solve the wrong problem you will have a hard time finding a solution that works. A special type of wrong problem is one that does not need to be solved. Does solving the problem really get you what you want? If it doesn't satisfy your end goal then forget about it and move on to something more productive.

Does Assumption of Approach cause the dilemma? If you go about achieving your goal in a different way does the dilemma disappear? For example:

> The battery of your portable electric refrigerator
> doesn't last for the whole camping trip; but,
> a bigger battery is too heavy to carry.

If you bring canned, or freeze dried food you don't need any battery or the portable electric refrigerator. The goal is to have food for the trip. Assuming you will keep the food refrigerated caused an unnecessary dilemma.

Exercise

Invert each word to reveal the assumptions and generalizations.

1. I want to ride my bicycle to work; but I smell bad when I perspire.

2. We need money to hire more teachers; but, the state can't afford to increase spending.

3. I need to lose weight; but, I don't have time to work out.

4. The wall has many stains; but, the landlord won't paint the wall.

5. My spouse wants to go surfing; but, I can't swim.

17.Example: Learning a Skill

Who wants to learn a skill? What desires are they trying to satisfy by performing the task of learning?

• Pass a test	• Entertainment
• Perform a task	• Share an experience
• Make a decision	
• Learn something else	
• Teach it	

Look at the different reasons for learning a skill. Are the reasons satisfied in the same way? Can we group them into functionally similar reasons? Are the differences qualitative or quantitative?

There appear to be two different types of reasons to learn a skill. The first is practical and the second is social.

The practical reasons for learning a skill are different from each other based on level of skill needed when complete. They can be ranked in order:

1. Able to make a decision

2. Perform a task

3. Pass a test

4. Learn another skill

5. Teach the subject

Even though the skill levels needed are ranked, there isn't a clear unit of measure so we can't quantitatively measure the differences. The difference is by qualitative type.

The social reasons, Entertainment and Share an Experience, are satisfied in different ways from the practical reasons. Even though learning the skill is desirable it is not essential to being entertained or sharing an experience. Enjoying the process is an essential Outcome for the social reasons. Enjoyment is beneficial but not required for the purely practical reasons to learn a skill so there is an overlap.

Since there are two different sets of Outcomes lets start with the practical reasons. Draw an Outcome diagram for the task. These Outcomes define successfully performing the task.

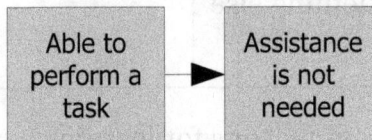

Able to perform a task → Assistance is not needed

Drawing 1: Learning a Skill Outcome Diagram

The Outcomes for Learning a Skill do not include all related Outcomes. Motivation to learn and perception of the process of learning are factors that should be considered but are not essential to the core set of Outcomes.

The Outcome diagram defines the Objects. The next step is to draw a Function diagram for the process of achieving the Outcomes. The last step of a Function diagram is achieving an Outcome.

Consider that you might need a Function diagram for each Outcome.

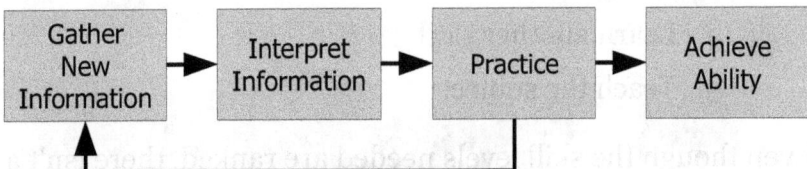

Gather New Information → Interpret Information → Practice → Achieve Ability

Drawing 2: Learning a Skill Function Diagram

Elements

Expand the Elements for each of the Outcomes and each of the Functions. Element expansion is a form of structured idea generation. It is not free-form. The goal is to list items for each of the 7 Elements, which are related to the Outcomes and Functions. This focuses your work and keeps it organized for finding patterns later.

Since many people are accustomed to brainstorming it can be helpful to temporarily skip the Outcome and Function diagram, and start by listing Elements. This can help people clarify their thinking before drawing the Function diagram.

You will need some knowledge of the subject matter you are innovating to be able to identify Elements. If you are innovating an engine you will need to understand some amount of mechanics.

Gather new information

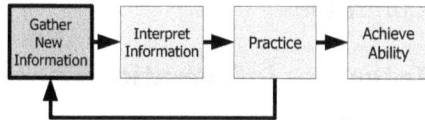

Objects

- Learner

- Information

Begin and End States

There are several combinations of these begin and End States. Depending on the purpose what is desired, undesired, and neutral changes.

- No information is gathered

- Related information is gathered

- Some of information is gathered

- All the information is gathered

- Extra information is gathered, not relevant

- Incorrect information is gathered, not factual

Actions

Read, Watch, Hear, Touch, Do it, Taste, Smell, Imagine, Measure

Tools
Books, magazines, websites, radio, TV, video, pictures, audio recordings, lectures, demonstrations, games, models, activities, samples, measurement devices, tests.

Conditions
Purpose, demographics, health of learner, other knowledge, past experiences, distractions, time available, comfort, emotions, format of information, language, physical environment, quality of information (incomplete or incorrect)

Resources
Medium of information, learner, other knowledge, emotions, physical environment, lecturer, friends, all of the Conditions.

Interpret information

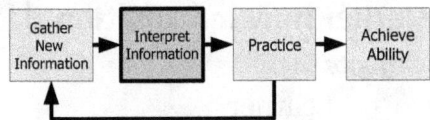

Gather New Information → Interpret Information → Practice → Achieve Ability

Objects
- Learner
- Information
- Meaning

Begin and End States
- No understanding
- Incorrect interpretation, misunderstood
- Partially understood
- Fully understood

Actions
Compare & contrast, Questions and answers, Thought experiment

Tools
Logic, restating in own words, lists, diagrams, conversations, email, text chat, phone, if...then statements, language, symbols

Conditions
Purpose, demographics, health of learner, other knowledge, past experiences, distractions, time available, comfort, emotions, format of information, language

Resources
All the Conditions, learner, emotions, physical environment, teacher, friends

Practice

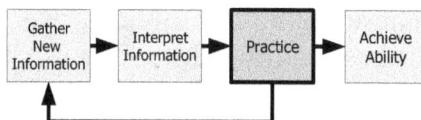

Objects
- Learner
- Skill level

Begin and End States
- No skill
- Some skill
- Full skill

Actions
Play, simulation, exercise, do the real thing, mental rehearsal

Tools
Games, simulation, real thing, simplified version of real thing, slow motion, weights, puzzles

Conditions
Difficulty of task, environment, health of learner

Resources
Objective measures of ability: time to complete an exercise, complexity of exercise completed, percentage of accurate results; measure of the difficulty of a type of practice: number of variables, amount of time given to complete task, number of mistakes allowed.

Achieve Ability

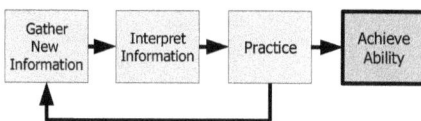

The final step in the Function diagram is satisfying both of the Outcomes of the Outcome diagram.

Achieve Ability is complete when the learner can perform the task and does not need assistance.

Objects

- Skill Level
- Learner

Begin and End States

There might be a quantitative measure for ability but it can be broken down into four functionally distinct levels.

- No ability
- Some ability
- Adequate ability
- Maximum ability

Actions

Do a task

Complete a test

Tools

Test, Questions, Measurement, Score, Mirror, Camera

Conditions

Time available, level of other abilities, number of skills being learned, wording of the test, time between receiving feedback

Resources

Feedback from others, results of previous attempts

Alternatives

Learner is involved in every Outcome in Learning a Skill; so, it makes sense to start finding Alternatives for Learner.

When I first tried to apply the Directions to Learner I was confused. I had difficulty figuring out what was a direct Learner versus a Stable Learner. The problem was I needed to chunk down Learner into Person and Learning. A learner is a person who is learning. Once I chunked down into the two parts it was easy to figure out. Chunking up and down is a useful approach to remember.

Person Alternatives

Person	+	-	=	→	~
1	Single person instructed Instructed once	Observer Prohibited Class or individual Learns how to find person who can do it Teach	Individual discovers skill One person always learns	Single learns until a point Single person learns existing information	Individual returns to learning Skills restored for an individual
m	Many people instructed Instructed many times	Many observers Learn to find many people who can do it Many prohibited people Group teaches	Group makes discovery Many people always learn	Many people learn until a point Many people learn existing information Learn existing information as a group	Group returns to learning Many people return to learning Skills are restored for many people
∞	Everyone instructed Continually instructed, never independent	Everyone learns by observing Everyone prohibited Everyone teaches	Everyone discovers for themselves Everyone always learns	Everyone learns until a point then stops Everyone learns existing information	Everyone returns to learning No one returns to learning

Learning Alternatives

Learning	+	-	=	→	~
1	Commanded one time Commanded for one task Commanded for one part of task	Individual doing other activity Doing one other activity Doing other activity once Forget Replace incorrect	Instinctive Already learned Apply existing knowledge Teach someone else	Skill becomes permanent Skill becomes permanent after single time Part of skill becomes permanent	Regain single skill Regain skill once Single reminder
m	Commanded for part of task Commanded many times	Doing many other activities Doing pieces of other activities Replace many incorrect Many steps to replace incorrect	Already know some of skill Already know many skills Teach many people Teach many skills	Many skills become permanent Skill becomes permanent after many times Skills become permanent in multiple parts	Regain many skills Regain skill many times Many reminders
∞	Commanded for everything Commanded for entire task Commanded until remembered	Doing every other activity Doing any other activity Do nothing, passive learning Continuously replace incorrect Replace all incorrect	Already know everything Already know nothing Already know anything Teach everything	All skills become permanent No skills become permanent Any skill becomes permanent Entire skill becomes permanent	Continually regaining skill Everyone regaining skills Regain any skill Reminders for everything Always reminded

Information Alternatives

Information	+	-	=	→	~
1	Next step Information to remember One more detail Custom information	Theory Grade / performance What not to do, contrast How to find information Reason for skill	Manual History Single fact	Revealed One gains acceptance Remembered after first time	Reminder, flash card Information changes once One part changes Uncertain
m	Multiple steps Some steps Many new things Many parts are new More information many things	Many theories Information about the information Multiple ways to find the information Partially correct Multiple grades	Multiple reminders Partial reminder Multiple facts Repeated information Partial history	Told many times before remembered Many things remembered Accepted as fact for many Conditions	Many parts change Changes many times Many parts uncertain
∞	All steps Always new information No steps Applies to everyone	All information about the information Totally false GPA Continual grading	Never reminded Always reminding Always same information Complete history	All information remembered Habit Becomes considered law	Information always changing Uncertain Unprovable

Meaning Alternatives

Meaning	+	-	=	→	~
1	Plain single meaning Meaningful in one Condition Increase meaning Told meaning Correct meaning	Indirect meaning Implied Opposite / Sarcasm One thing unknown Confused about one thing	Same meaning Doesn't change for one Condition One meaning stays the same	Takes time to understand	Situational meaning Meaning changes once Understands after one error
m	Plain meaning multiple Conditions Increases meaning multiple Conditions Many things increase meaning	Multiple implications Contradictory meanings Partially wrong meaning Wrong meaning many things	Same meaning many Conditions Many meaning stay the same Parts of meaning stay the same Partially understood	Multiple exposures to understand Multiple parts before understanding Part of information before understanding	Corrects meaning many times/ways Meaning changes many Conditions Parts change meaning
∞	No meaning Always increasing meaning Increase meaning everything	Unknown meaning Meaning is hidden Totally confused Totally wrong	Same meaning all situations Always understood	Understood by everyone Needs all to understand Understands everything	Always relearn Meaning constantly changing Everything changes meaning Always becomes clear again

Skill Level Alternatives

Skill Level	+	-	=	→	~
1	Skill level improves once One part of skill improves	Skill decreases Other skill change Task becomes easier One part of task becomes harder (exercise)	Single skill level stays the same Skill same in one situation	One skill increases to point (learn once) Skill increases to a point for one Condition	Skill level fluctuates once One skill level fluctuates
m	Many skills improve Skill improves many times Skill partially improves	Many other skills change Skill decreases many times Parts of task become harder Parts of task become easier	Partial skill level stays the same Multiple skill levels stay the same Skill same in many situations	Multiple skill levels increase to point Skill plateaus multiple times	Skill level fluctuates many times Many skill levels fluctuate
∞	Skill level always improves	Completely loses skill Improves all other skills Task eliminated	Skill level never changes Skill same in all situations	Maximum skill level achieved All skills increased to a point Become expert in all aspects	Skill level never consistent Continuous practice needed

Gather Information Alternatives

Gather information	+	-	=	→	~
1	Do it, experience, see yourself	Read, told, watch video, theory	Fixed belief, one thing, one time Consistent once	Confirm belief once	Single change or difference Average one variable
m	Repeat experience Experience many things directly	Many indirect sources Indirectly experience many things Theory	Fixed belief, many things Consistent many times	Confirm belief many times Confirm many beliefs	Many changes or differences Average many variables Moving average
∞	Experience everything Experience anything	No direct experience	Believes everything, never changes	Confirm all beliefs	All differences Rate of change

Practice Alternatives

Practice	+	-	=	→	~
1	Real thing once	Imagine, simulation	One type of practice	Single Test	Rehab
m	Real thing many times Parts of real	Simulate multiple aspects	Do same thing many times Repeat different parts	Multiple tests	Occasionally different Consistency
∞	Always real Any real	Simulate all aspects	Same thing every time Habit	Continually testing Test everything	Constantly changing

Achieve Ability Alternatives

Achieve ability	+	-	=	→	~
1	Do it once First try	Simulation once Lose ability once	Complete practice once	Test completed once	Re-certification
m	Done many times Do pieces	Multiple simulations Lose many abilities	Complete practice multiple times	Multiple tests completed	Many re-certifications
∞	Done all aspects	All aspects simulated Any aspect simulated Lose all ability Lose any ability	Complete all practice	All tests completed Perfect score on test	Test before each time

18.Example: Bicycle

Bicycle is a type of transportation. The basic Outcomes for all forms of transportation are the same. There are only two Outcomes, an item is at one location then is at a different location.

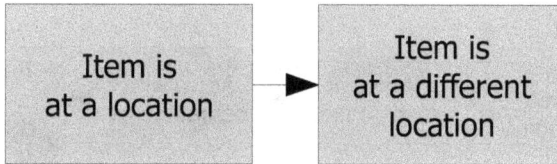

Drawing 3: High-level Outcomes for Transportation

Even though the most basic Outcome diagram has only two Outcomes there are many other performance Outcomes to achieve the ideal for transportation.

Transport what you want,
when you want, where you want,
the way you want,
with what and whom you want,
for the price you want with no hassle.

- Where the item is being moved to and from?
- When you start to transport the item? Start time.
- When the item arrives?
- Cost: Length of time needed to transport the item is a cost.
- Cost: Damage from a lack of safety is a cost.
- Hassle: Lack of safety also causes hassle.
- Cost: Energy needed to move the item is a cost.
- Cost: Pollution from transportation is a cost.
- Hassle: Anything that reduces comfort is a hassle.
- What item is being transported?
- Who wants the item transported?
- With: Combinations of items being transported.

The chunked down or zoomed in Outcome diagram looks like this:

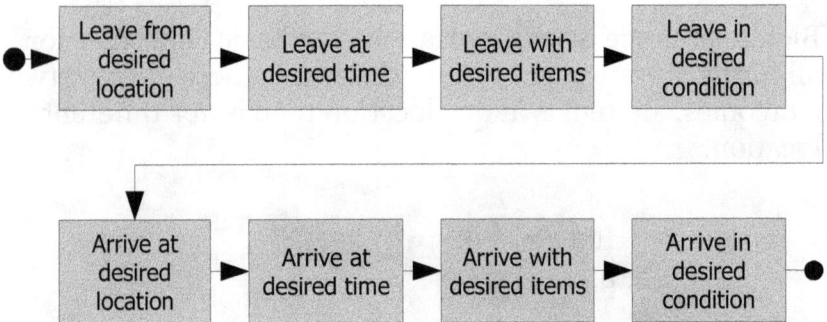

Drawing 4: Chunked down Outcomes for Transportation

Notice that the first 4 Outcomes are a more detailed description of "Item is at a location" and the second 4 Outcomes are a more detailed description of "Item is at a different location".

I've left out of the diagram the cost of pollution and energy because it's not part of the required Outcomes to achieve the goal of transportation. Those extra Outcomes are important fertile areas of innovation.

Another very important point to consider is the purpose of transportation. The basic Outcome of transportation is to move an item from one location to a different location. Often people will perform a task because it satisfies another desire. Many people ride bicycles for exercise or entertainment. Optimizing the different Outcomes for exercise or entertainment is very different from riding a bicycle purely for transportation.

A perfect example of the Outcomes being different based on the purpose is a stationary exercise bicycle. A stationary bicycle is useless for transportation but ideal for many Conditions of exercise or entertainment.

> *Determine the purpose*
> *before drawing an Outcomes diagram.*

Functions

The Functions of a bicycle are determined by the Outcomes. A stationary exercise bicycle has different Functions than a bicycle used for transportation. Both share some Functions such as acquiring energy from the user.

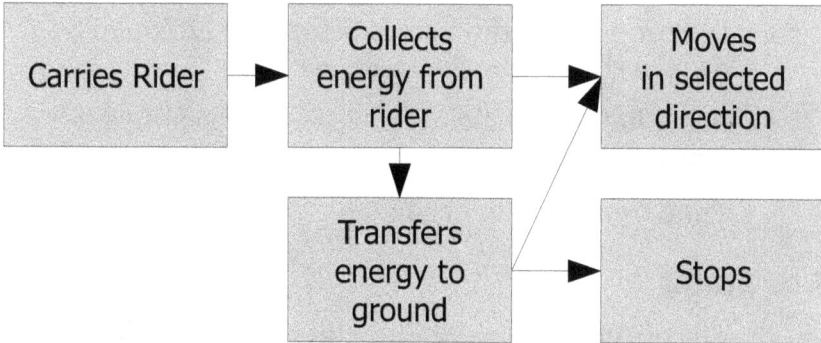

Drawing 5: Bicycle Function Diagram

Even though a stationary bicycle doesn't move the user still needs it to stop and wants it pointed in the desired direction. Also the energy isn't transferred to the ground but something must be done with the energy collected from the user pedaling.

Elements

The ideal statement can help identify the Elements. Who and what are Objects. Where and when are Conditions or Begin and End States. Cost and hassle are undesired End States.

Objects

- Location of item. This is where the item currently is located. Transporting the item changes the location of the item.

- Item being transported

- Health of person transported

- Comfort of person transported

- Amount needed to transport
- Maximum energy level needed to transport
- Energy available for transporting

Begin States

- Location where the item is before the Action of transporting is the Begin State
- Being healthy and undamaged is a typical Begin State
- Time transporting begins

End States

- The destination is the End State of the location of the item.
- An item being damaged or unhealthy is an undesired End State.
- Tired, undesired for transportation. Possibly desired for exercise.
- Wet from perspiration, undesired.
- Time transporting ends
  - On-time, desirable
  - Early, desirable, neutral
  - Late, undesirable
- Length of time to transport

Actions

- Move
- Stop
- Turn
- Rest

- Lean
- Park
- Mount / Dismount

Conditions

- Start time can affect the end time, safety, etc.
- End time
- Location where the item is moving. The location Condition is a different concept from the location Object. Condition affects the ability of being able to change the Object. Transporting the item to a location that is far away will affect the ability to transport it.

Resources

There are many Resources available in transportation including: passenger, weather, other vehicles, gravity, time of day, surface of the road, etc.

Components

Once you have the Functions defined you can perform the Function using Components. The 15 Alternatives and 7 Elements also apply to Components so you can start with an existing device like a bicycle and find Alternatives for each Component.

A bicycle has many Components. Lets look at 9 of the major Components.

· wheels	· seat	· brakes
· tires	· frame	· pedals
· handle bars	· gears	· forks

Objects for wheel:

Size, shape, weight, solid, spoked, material

Wheel	+	-	=	→	~
1	Single wheel directly moves bicycle Single wheel, unicycle Wheel is added to the bicycle.	Single indirect wheel Wheel drives treads Single Other than wheel, ski Other part of the bicycle	Same Keep Prevent One Once Wheel stays with the bicycle, welded on	Becomes a single wheel, once One wheel stabilizes, once, one condition	Restore Repair Replace One wheel, once, one condition
m	Many wheels directly move bicycle (2 wheel drive) Many wheels (tricycle, quad-cycle, etc) Partial wheel,	Indirect, wheel not part of bicycle. Road is wheels like a conveyor. Other Many other, skis Partial	Many same, multiple fixed wheels Partial same, part of wheel is fixed. Wheel doesn't change many times, some conditions	Wheel stabilizes many times, many conditions, many wheels Becomes many wheels Becomes a wheel many times, many conditions Becomes part of a wheel	Wheel repairs many times, or conditions Replace part of wheel Wheel changeable, many options
∞	All wheel bicycle (sphere like Illustration 29: Cage keeps tigers out) Any No wheel	Any indirect, wheel drive treads, or propeller, etc. All indirect Any other, choose any option All other, all options included	Any wheel stable Wheel always same, last for lifetime No wheel same, customized	Becomes any wheel, any condition Becomes all wheel(s) Becomes no wheel: track, float	Any wheel repaired All wheels repaired No wheel repairs, see Keep Stable

19.Combinations

Combinations of Alternatives find the huge numbers of
organized ideas suitable for continually lower risk and high
return on investment innovations. A good place to start is
by finding combinations between an Object and Action.
This will reveal 225 combinations.

			B														
			1					m					∞				
			+	-	=	→	~	+	-	=	→	~	+	-	=	→	~
A	1	+															
		-															
		=															
		→															
		~															
	m	+															
		-															
		=															
		→															
		~															
	∞	+															
		-															
		=															
		→															
		~															

This quickly results in extremely large numbers of
combinations. Using only one example for each of the 7
Elements for one Outcome results in $15^7 = 170,859,375$
combinations. With 7 Outcomes the combinations increase
to a minimum of 4.25 e+57. That is 425 followed by 55
zeros.

You do not need to explore every combination. Products innovate if they satisfy the emerging expectations. Trying to build or sell products that are too far ahead of demand or technology will produce poor results. Planning 6 generations of products into the future is usually ideal for staying ahead of demand and not wasting effort on unrealistic concepts.

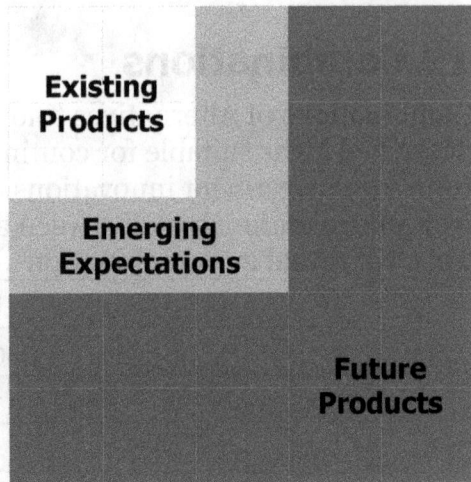

Existing Products

Emerging Expectations

Future Products

Since combinations are made by multiplying Outcomes, Elements, and Alternatives you can easily find a set of combinations when needed. All the combinations are neatly organized and easily accessible.

For new product innovation you want to make sure your design allows you to use as many of the most desirable combinations as possible. You can determine this without actually looking at every individual combination. Just looking at unusual combinations to test if those are possible can often be enough to make a decision about a design approach.

For more advanced analysis you can use sampling techniques, such as Taguchi[9], to calculate with high confidence that your design covers the entire idea space.

Combinations are very helpful for problem solving. For problem solving you are not interested in all the combinations, just finding a good one as quickly as possible. If the Direct approach is not working you can look at the Indirect, Keep Stable, Make Stable, or Return to Stable. This format creates a checklist so you know you are actually thinking of new ideas and not just going in circles.

---

9   Covered in Strategist

You can also focus on one set of approaches at a time. This allows you to rapidly narrow your thinking to the most productive areas.

For problem solving you can often find a suitable solution without looking at all the 15 Alternatives. When you expanded the Elements you likely came up with many Actions, Tools, Conditions, and Resources for each Object. You can look at combinations between these. I find that looking at Conditions is an effective way to resolve troublesome dilemmas. You can do that by setting up a table of Actions and Conditions.

Consider that you listed 5 Actions and 5 Conditions. That is 25 combinations.

	Action 1	Action 2	Action 3	Action 4	Action 5
Condition 1					
Condition 2					
Condition 3					
Condition 4					
Condition 5					

You can do the same thing for all the Elements. You can also chunk down into each combination using Alternatives. So, in that there are 225 Alternatives for each Element combination. In this example of 5 Conditions and 5 Actions there are 5,625 Alternatives. You should not need to explore all of those to find a suitable solution.

20.Innovation Quotient

Predictive Innovation allows you to map the entire idea space for a concept. This means you can calculate the percentage of the idea space open for innovation or covered by your design. That percentage is the Innovation Quotient. A perfect Innovation Quotient is 100%.

The simple version of the Innovation Quotient is:

$$IQ = \frac{Ideas\ Covered}{Total\ Space}$$

This allows you to compare the potential of two different idea spaces or two different approaches to address an idea space.

The simple version is good for getting a quick-rough estimate of the innovation potential of a market or design. The more detailed approach to calculating the Innovation Quotient can:

- quantify risk

- compare the value of different designs

- calculate depreciation for an innovation

Innovation Quotients are beyond the scope of Core Skills and are only mentioned to make you aware of additional capabilities of Predictive Innovation.

Visit www.PredictiveInnovation.com to learn more about creating business models, designing strategies, and calculating advanced Innovation Quotients.

21.Predicting

An idea is innovative when it is what the customer wants and it is profitably delivered. Profitable is not just financial for the person selling it. It must better satisfy one or more Outcomes while satisfying all other Outcomes at least as well as existing products. Giving up satisfaction is a cost that makes a product non-profitable to users. This is often a problem with new technology.

Even if a product would otherwise be desired it can fail to innovate because it is too soon or too late.

	Too Soon	Too Late
What is wanted	· Required Components not available · Cost too much · Existing products satisfy current desires	· Other options available
How to make it	· Technology not advanced · Poor quality	· Profit margin too low

Timing is difficult since it depends on actions of human beings. Predictive Innovation does not claim to predict dates. Predictive Innovation predicts sequences of innovations. The invention of the wheel, fire, and steel must happen before the automobile. Additionally, if customers are not using the existing products to the full potential they will not see value in something that is better. People who live on a small self-sufficient island don't need automobiles. The advantage of speed is not worth the investment or costs. If there isn't a source of fuel an automobile would be worthless.

So there is a sequence of innovations. These sequences can be predicted and the signs recognized. Since all innovations are moving towards the ideal there is a natural progression. This progression can be seen in the 15-Alternatives.

	Direct	Indirect	Keep Stable	Make Stable	Return to Stable
Single					
Multiple					
Continuous					

Innovations tend to start as Single Direct Alternatives then move towards a Continuous Stable Alternative. Innovations can progress towards any of the 3-Stable Alternatives to become ideal.

The ideal product always has the desired State. This would suggest the natural progression is from Return to Stable, to Make Stable, and finally Keep Stable. At the very last step in the ideal progression this is likely to be true but during the many steps towards the ideal the progression of Stable Alternatives may follow a different order. Different technological advancements at the point when a Stable Alternative is the next step can change which type of Stable is next on the path but the tendency is towards one of the Stable Alternatives and always towards a Continuous Alternative.

Predicting Process

The process for predicting innovations has four steps

1. Diagram the Outcomes
2. List the Ideal State for each Outcome
3. Divide the range of improvements into Functional Distinctions
4. Map the steps covering the idea space

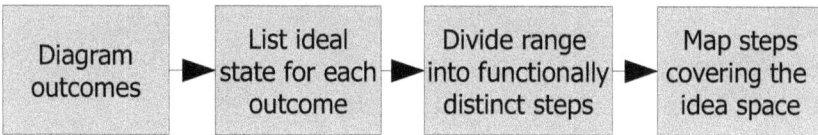

Diagram outcomes	→	List ideal state for each outcome	→	Divide range into functionally distinct steps	→	Map steps covering the idea space

Drawing 6: Predicting Process

1. Diagram Outcomes

The first step is to diagram the Outcomes. Start with the user core Outcomes then diagram the Functions and breakdown each Function into its Outcomes. Since innovations may change the steps required to achieve the Outcomes you may need to make several versions of the Function diagrams to cover the entire range from the current product to the ideal.

2. Ideal States

The second step is to list the Ideal State for each Outcome. Each Outcome has an Ideal State and each Function for achieving the Outcome has a set of Outcomes, each with Ideal States for performing the Function. These are the goals to guide all the innovations.

Using the 5 directions of the Alternatives we find the different ways to achieve an Ideal State.

+	-	=	→	~
Maximize	Minimize	Match	Minimize amount of difference	Minimize frequency of difference
		Avoid	Maximize difference of amount	Maximize frequency of difference

Maximizing a State increases it to the most possible or the most with a Functional Distinction.

Minimizing a State makes it as close to zero or not happening as possible. Under some situations a negative amount might be possible. For example: instead of just reducing waste to zero you sell the waste for a profit. If you have used the indirect to turn a negative into a positive it is best to redraw the Outcome diagram so that the negative-indirect is the positive-direct and maximize that State. This will also reveal a new set of stable options.

Matching is a form of stable. Matching minimizes the difference from the ideal either in frequency or amount.

Avoiding is the indirect form of stable. Avoiding maximizes the difference from the ideal either in frequency or amount.

Each step on each of the innovation paths is a Functional Distinction of what and how. Since these branch from an existing product they have similarities and in this way considered adjacent in a multidimensional idea space.

3. Functionally Distinct Steps

The third step is to break the range of improvements into Functional Distinctions. Its usually not possible to jump to the end Ideal State so you must break down the path between what is available now and the ideal into steps of what can be delivered and will be accepted. Each functionally distinct desired step is an innovation closer to the ideal.

Example: Wagon wheel

A wagon wheel starts as a simple wooden circle with an axle. The solid wooden wheel is uncomfortable, heavy, and tends to fling mud on a passenger. This limits how fast the wagon can travel.

Adding a fender to the wagon prevents mud from being flung onto the passengers. This allows the wagon to travel a little faster but it is too uncomfortable and hard to control to meaningfully increase the speed.

The wheel can be made lighter by using spokes instead of the solid wooden circle. The spokes would tend to fling more mud but the fender prevents the mud from hitting the passenger so at this point the change is an innovation where it would not be before the fender. The lighter wheels make the wagon easier to control allowing it to move faster. This also would tend to fling more mud but the fender prevents it from hitting the passenger. A faster moving wagon is more uncomfortable so the speed is still limited.

The next innovation is springs but this requires a new technology of steel to make the springs. Adding springs would make the wagon heavier and harder to control but the spoked wheels are lighter and make up for the difference and springs make it more comfortable at faster speeds. Since the driver is not shaken as much the wagon is also more controllable. Steel is much stronger than wood so stronger wheels that weigh less can be made improving control and speed.

Finally tires are added increasing control, speed, and comfort. Tires are not possible until vulcanized rubber is developed.

The tire could have been added to the solid wooden wheel but the slow speed and general rough ride would not make the benefit of the tire noticeable.

The spring is a separate Component from the wheel and the fender. The spring would improve comfort but add weight making the wagon harder to control. It would allow the wagon to move faster but that would fling more mud on the passenger. The benefits of the spring are not appreciated without the improvements of the fender and spoked wheel.

The changes improved three different Outcomes by changing one Component twice and adding two new Components. Two enabling technologies were required to make the improvements.

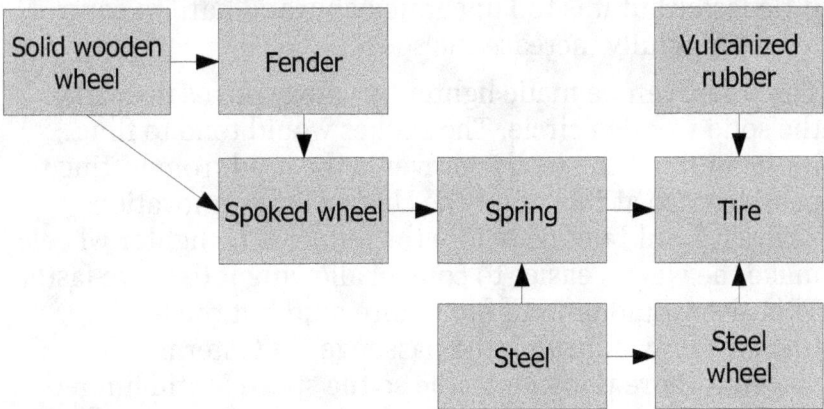

Drawing 7: Wheel stages of innovation

All of these incremental improvements lead to the conditions needed for the "what" and "how" of an automobile.

4. Map Steps Covering the Idea Space

The fourth step is to map the steps covering the idea space. There isn't just one path to the ideal product. There are many profitable innovations covering the idea space. Your goal as an innovator is to deliver as many of those innovations as you can while progressing toward the ideal.

Future Map

The combination of all the steps towards the ideal forms a map of a family of products and services. The region extending out from the existing products are covered by the emerging expectations. A product will fail to innovate if it is attempted too soon so you should focus on a range of 5-6 product generations. These will be connected like the example of the wagon wheel. Each improvement makes other improvements possible. This becomes like bowling pins. The first pin knocks down those behind it, which in turn knock down more causing a cascade knocking all of them down. When you properly arrange the sequence of connections between innovations your profits increase and the effort decreases.

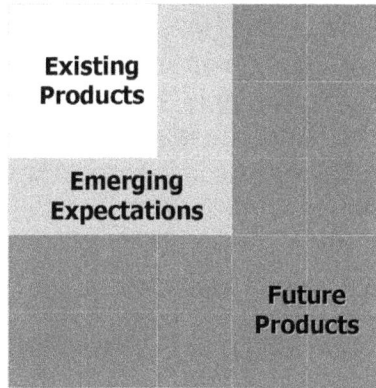

Creating future maps is covered in detail in Strategist training.

Under-served Outcomes

Innovations satisfy the currently under-served Outcomes. Each new innovation increases the level of satisfaction for one or more Outcomes. Customers become accustomed to this new level and begin to expect the new level as the minimum. New innovations must do more or better for the same users in the same scenario.

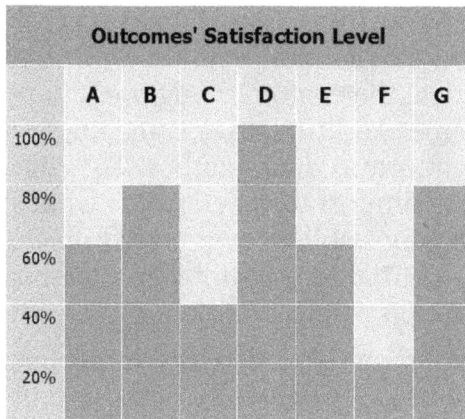

Satisfaction levels for Outcomes can be measured by surveying users with a 5-point scale. This is <u>not the typical marketing measurement</u>. The survey is measuring the level the Outcome is satisfied and not how much they like a feature. It is also important to whenever possible use objective units to measure satisfaction such as meters, dollars, or numbers of occurrence of an event.

How satisfied are you with your ability to...?	Not satisfied 1	Somewhat satisfied 2	Satisfied 3	Very satisfied 4	Extremely satisfied 5
Outcome XYZ	☐	☐	☐	☐	☐

An example of objective 5-point scale could be applied to price. Free is the ideal price for a product that is not purchased solely for status. If the current price is $100 you could break down the range between $0 and $100 into a 5-point scale.

Which price are you willing to pay to be able to ...?	$76 - $100	$51 - $75	$26 - $50	$1 - $25	$0.00
Outcome XYZ	☐	☐	☐	☐	☐

Measuring Satisfaction Levels is not enough. Even though the satisfaction level for an Outcome might be far from the ideal the customer might not consider it important at this time. Additionally, people might rank one Outcome more important than another. The combination or satisfaction and importance determine what customers will want next. It is possible to over-satisfy an Outcome. This creates the potential for disruptive innovation. A lesser but lower cost option would be acceptable to potential customers.

You must also measure Importance Level. This can be done with a 5-point scale. When combined with the Satisfaction Level you can assess the amount and urgency for improving an Outcome.

How important is it for you to be able to...?	Not important 1	Somewhat important 2	Important 3	Very important 4	Extremely important 5
Outcome XYZ	☐	☐	☐	☐	☐

Plotting Satisfaction Level and Importance Level on a graph makes an Opportunity Landscape. This is a concise graphical representation of the innovation potential of a product or market.

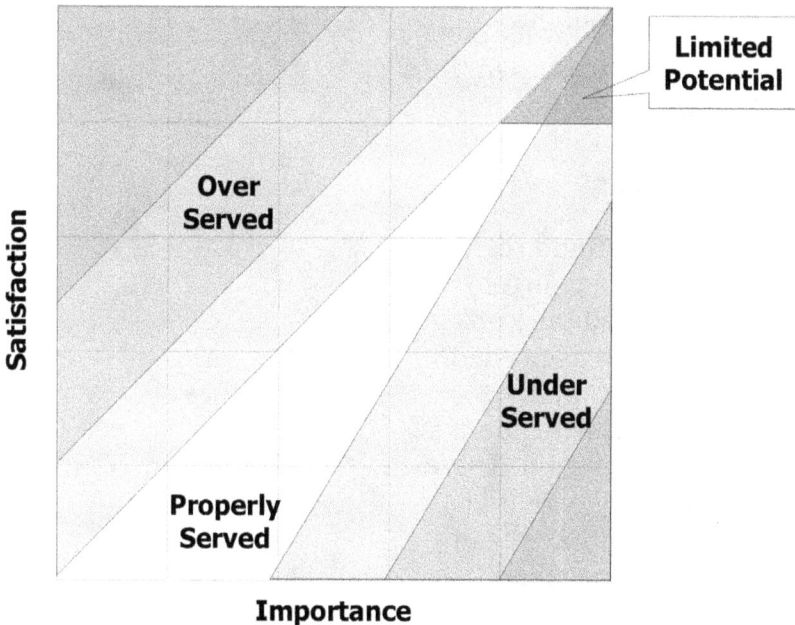

Illustration 56: Opportunity Landscape

There are four regions of the Opportunity Landscape. You can determine how to focus your innovation activities based on the region the majority of Outcomes appear.

New Market

The lower right hand section of the chart show Outcomes that currently satisfied less than desired and customers view as important. These under-served Outcomes represent opportunities for improvement. New markets have many Outcomes in the under-served region.

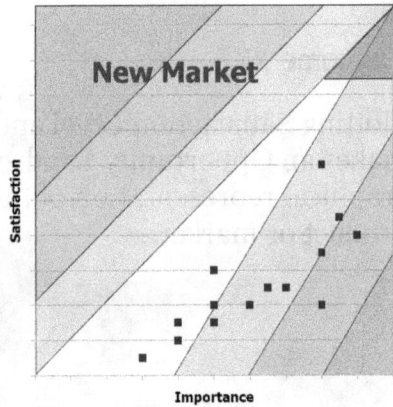

Disruption Risk

The upper left hand region is Outcomes that current products exceed the level customers view as needed. If a product has many Outcomes in this region it is at risk for disruption. There are likely many potential customers who have been priced out of the market or who would gladly accept a lesser product if it satisfied a different Outcome or cost less.

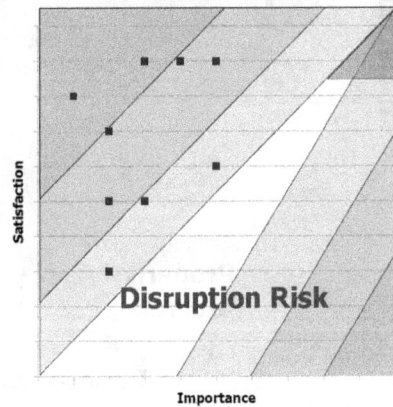

Limited Potential

The upper right hand corner is the Limited Potential region. Outcomes in the Limited Potential region are currently satisfied but are extremely important. You can't increase the satisfaction but if you reduce the level of satisfaction customers will be upset. As markets mature Outcomes tend towards this region. Products with the majority of Outcomes in this region tend to suffer from commodity pricing since there is little potential for improvement in other ways. You need to find other markets before your products end up in the Limited Potential region.

Find Other Markets

The center band extending from the lower left to the upper right is the Properly Served region. Your goal as an innovator is to keep all the Outcomes in the Properly Served region. When you have all the Outcomes in this region you should explore new markets.

To maximize profits you should keep the Outcomes in the Properly Served and have another market developed before the Outcomes move into the Limited Potential region.

The difference between the Satisfaction Level and the Importance for an Outcome is the Opportunity Score.

$$Opportunity\ Score_i = \left| Importance_i - Satisfaction_i \right|$$

The greater the difference the more opportunity for innovation. This can either be done by increasing the Satisfaction Level for under-served Outcomes or delivering a trimmed down version for products with over-served Outcomes.

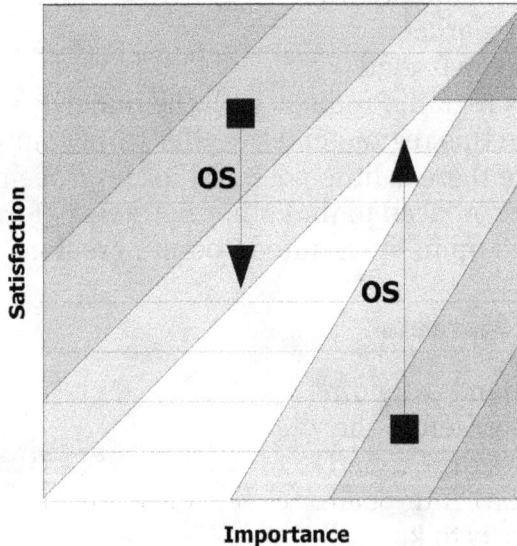

Illustration 57: Opportunity Score

When comparing different markets or products, sum the Opportunity Scores for all the Outcomes to find an Overall Opportunity Score. Markets or products with a higher Overall Opportunity Score offer great potential for innovation.

$$Overall Opportunity\ Score = \sum_{i=1}^{n} \left| Importance_i - Satisfaction_i \right|$$

The Opportunities Score shows you how far the Outcomes are from the Properly Served region.

Breakthrough vs. Incremental Innovation

Many people put a great deal of emphasis on trying to create breakthrough innovations. This stems from the misplaced belief that innovations are difficult to find. Predictive Innovation reveals the entire idea space so you can reliably find collections of highly profitable innovations when needed.

You can profit from either breakthrough or incremental innovations. Neither is inherently better. The proper strategy is to ideally time the innovations to maximize profit margins.

There is a time for harvesting incremental innovations and a time for sowing a new field with a breakthrough.

Incremental Innovations	Breakthrough Innovations
• Better or cheaper • More of the same	• Do something previously not possible • Functionally different

Remember that the definition of innovation is:

Profitably satisfy unmet desires

As long as you are better satisfying desires you are innovating. Financial profits and customer satisfaction profits can be achieved either way.

Since breakthroughs are functionally different that means they use a different Alternative or satisfy a previously ignored Outcome.

22.Summary

Predictive Innovation completely changes what is possible for innovation and problem solving. The systematic approach helps you analyze anything, not just businesses. The more you practice Predictive Innovation the more uses you will find.

Hopefully the explanations and many examples in this book are enough for you to begin using Predictive Innovation on your own. Too help you gain a deeper understanding more quickly we offer training. To see the current training options, visit www.PredictiveInnovation.com

Being able to reliably predict customers emerging expectations and ways of satisfying those expectations opens up a wide variety of new business models and strategies.

Now that you know the basics of Predictive Innovation I recommend reading "The Mind of the Startup Strategist" by Len Kaplan, ISBN 978-0-557-04498-6. This book presents 12 strategies to maximize profits and minimize the risks facing any new product and especially a startup business. These strategies were developed using Predictive Innovation and can only be performed if you know how to use Predictive Innovation. This can be your secret advantage.

We constantly research new and better techniques and ways to apply Predictive Innovation. Sign up for a free newsletter to receive updates on the newest developments.

Next Step
- Attend Practitioner Workshop
- Sign up for the newsletter

23.Glossary

Action: One of the 7 Elements of an Outcome or Function. Action is performed to cause the End State.

Actor: A person who has desires needing innovation or who makes innovations. Actors are divided into two types Customer and Innovator, which are subdivided into User, Buyer, Payer, Communicator, Designer, Maker, and Seller.

Alternative: There are 15 Alternative approaches to achieve any Outcome or Function. The 15 Alternatives are organized into a 3x5 Grid with rows: Single, Multiple, and Continuous; and columns: Direct, Indirect, Keep Stable, Make Stable, and Return to Stable.

Assumption of Approach: Is assuming there are no other ways of achieving the result. Using the 15 Alternatives will help you avoid making Assumptions of Approach.

Assumption of Result: When the purpose is not accurately defined the undesired results are assumed to be the goal.

Begin State: One of the 7 Elements of an Outcome or Function. The State of the Object before the action occurs.

Buyer: The Actor who makes the decision to buy the product or service. A buyer can be one or more different people.

Communicator: The Actor who gathers and transmits the information of the desires of the customer and the benefits of the product or service. The communicator is the link between the innovator and customer.

Component: The physical parts or computer code used to make a product. Components are the real world items that perform the Functions of a product or service.

Condition: One of the 7 Elements of an Outcome or Function. Condition is a State that affects the results of the action trying to achieve the End State.

Continuous: One of the 3 scales of the Alternatives Grid. Continuous

Customer: The person who uses, buys, and pays for a product or service. A customer may be a single person or different people who perform the roles of Users, Buyer, and Payer.

Designer: The Actor who forms the information needed to build a product or perform a service.

Desire: Desires are what an Actor wants in a particular Scenario. Desires are subjective and usually emotionally based.

Dilemma: When there are two desired results and it seems that the only way to improve one is to make the other worse.

Dimension: A range of properties or categories for describing an object.

Direct: One of the 5 directions of the Alternatives Grid. Direct actions are performed on the Object and stop having effect when the action is stopped.

Direction: The 5 columns of the Alternatives Grid: Direct, Indirect, Keep Stable, Make Stable, and Return to Stable.

Element: The 7 fundamental parts of an Outcome or Function: Objects, Begin States, End States, Actions, Tools, Conditions, and Resources.

Emotional Assumption: Beliefs formed to confirm the emotional state.

End State: The State of the Object after the action has occurred.

Fractal: Infinite complexity resulting from repeated simple rules. Benoît Mandelbrot is the mathematician credited with describing the concept of a fractal. Fractal mathematics describe many natural structures and occurrences.

Function: Function is the change needed to achieve a desire. Innovations perform Functions to satisfy desires. A Function is similar to an Outcome but is focused on the action rather than the States.

Function Diagram: Graphical representation of the process of achieving a goal, also known as a flow chart.

Functional Distinction: A difference that affects the results generated or meaningfully alters the way something is done so as to make something possible that previously was not possible.

Generalization: Assuming something is the same or applies in different situations. Accurate generalizations are useful for finding similarities but inaccurate or excess generalizations can lead to incorrect conclusions.

Hyper Cube: An asymmetric multidimensional data set. Unlike a symmetric multidimensional data set where there is a value for each combination of dimensions, a hypercube might have combinations without data. An example is a hypercube of states, cities, and streets. Not all cities will have all the same street names.

Indirect: One of the directions of the Alternatives Grid. Indirect is the opposite or different approach. If the direct approach is adding more, indirect is removing to have less. If the direct is the material then the indirect is Tool or environment or something else that is not the direct approach.

Keep Stable: The direction of the Alternatives Grid that starts with the desired States and maintain that State.

Make Stable: The directions of the Alternatives Grid where the State starts in an undesired State then changed to become a stable desired State.

Maker: The Actor who makes the product or performs the service to achieve the innovation.

Morphological Analysis: A thinking system created by Fritz Zwicky, noted physicist, based on breaking a problem down into parts to allow you do find all the combinations.

Multidimensional: Having many dimensions. Physical objects have 3 spatial dimensions. Many other physical and non-physical dimensions can be used to describe an object such as color, weight, price, or age.

Multiple: One of the scales of the Alternatives Grid. Multiple is more than one and less than continuous or infinite. Multiple scale can be applied to anything.

NLP: Neuro-Linguistic Programming, a method for understanding and altering mental states and reactions.

Object: The focus of innovation or problem solving. The thing that needs to change to achieve the desired State.

Outcome: Objective State that results from a cause. Used to define the criteria for satisfying desires. Consists of Object, Begin States, End States, Actions, Tools, Conditions, and Resources. The fundamental building block of innovation.

Outcome Driven: Activities guided by achieving result. Focusing on the States needed to achieve the desired goal.

Outcome Diagram: Graphical representation of the criteria required to satisfy a desire.

Paradigm: A set of assumptions and beliefs that guide behavior.

Payer: The Actor who pays for or provides the materials and labor needed to make the innovation.

Purpose: The goal of using a product or service. What the user wants to achieve. Often expressed in subjective terms.

Resource: Anything in the environment that can be used to achieve the desired State.

Return to Stable: One of the five directions of the Alternatives Grid. Return to Stable allows the desired State to change but returns to the desired State.

Scale: The three rows of the 3x5 Alternatives Grid consisting of Single, Multiple, and Continuous. Each of the three scales is functionally distinct from the others.

Scenario: All the information relating to an Actor's particular set of desires. Described by an IF...THEN statement.

Single: One of the three scales of the Alternatives Grid. Single is described by words such as: one, first, only, and unique.

State: State is the value of an Object such as color, size, weight, or the occurrence of an event.

Tool: Tool is directly used to perform an Action.

User: User is the person who uses the product. User is one of the Actors that make up the three roles of a customer. Also see: Actor, payer, & buyer.

www.ingramcontent.com/pod-product-compliance
Lightning Source LLC
Chambersburg PA
CBHW061310220326
41599CB00026B/4815